THEMES
for early years

CLOTHES

ANNE PIPER

THEMES
for early years

Author Anne Piper
Editor Lorna Gilbert
Assistant editor Lesley Sudlow
Series designer Lynne Joesbury
Designer Clare Brewer
Illustrations Angie Sage
Cover Lynne Joesbury
Action Rhymes, Poems and Stories compiled by Jackie Andrews
Songs compiled by Peter Morrell
Assemblies chapter by Lesley Prior
Designed using Adobe Pagemaker

Published by Scholastic Ltd, Villiers House, Clarendon Avenue, Leamington Spa, Warwickshire CV32 5PR

© 1998 Scholastic Ltd Text © 1998
1 2 3 4 5 6 7 8 9   8 9 0 1 2 3 4 5 6 7

The publishers gratefully acknowledge permission to reproduce the following copyright material:
Jackie Andrews for the use of the retelling of the Brothers Grimm story of 'The Elves and the Shoemaker' © 1998, Jackie Andrews, previously unpublished; **Clive Barnwell** for the use of 'Rub-A-Dub-A-Dub' and 'The Shoe Shop' © 1998, Clive Barnwell, previously unpublished; **Ann Bryant** for the use of 'Sparkling Jewels for Sale' © 1998, Ann Bryant, previously unpublished; **Sue Cowling** for the use of 'Picking Up The Clothes', 'Socks' and 'Burger Bar Girl' © 1998, Sue Cowling, previously unpublished; **Gina Douthwaite** for the use of 'Lost Sock' © 1998, Gina Douthwaite, previously unpublished; **John Foster** for the use of 'How Did Your Mum Do The Washing, Gran?' © 1998, previously unpublished; **Jan Holdstock** for the use of 'Uniforms' and 'A Big Ball of Wool' © 1998, Jan Holdstock, previously unpublished; **Karen King** for the use of 'The Red Sock' © 1998, Karen King, previously unpublished; **Ladybird Books Ltd** for the use of 'The Emperor's New Clothes' a retelling of the Hans Christian Andersen story by Audrey Daly from *Favourite Tales* © 1993, Audrey Daly (1993, Ladybird Books Ltd); **Ian Larmont** for the use of 'Second Best' © 1998, Ian Larmont, previously unpublished; **Johanne Levy** for the use of 'Me and My Clothes' © 1998, Johanne Levy, previously unpublished; **Wes Magee** for the use of 'Who Am I?' © 1998, Wes Magee, previously unpublished; **Tony Mitton** for the use of 'My Jumper', 'Grown Out Of' and 'Clumsy Giant Gets Up' © 1998, Tony Mitton, previously unpublished; **Barbara Moore** for the use of 'Clothes for a Cold Day' © 1998, Barbara Moore, previously unpublished; **Belinda Morley** for the use of 'Hooray for Clothes' © 1998, Belinda Morley, previously unpublished; **Peter Morrell** for the arrangement of the traditional songs of 'Aiken Drum' and 'Poor Jenny Sits A-Weeping' © 1998, Peter Morrell, previously unpublished; **Judith Nicholls** for 'Let's Do The Flip-Flop Frolic' © 1998, Judith Nicholls, previously unpublished and 'Pssst!' from *Popcorn Pie* by Judith Nicholls © 1988, Judith Nicholls (1989, Mary Glasgow Publications); **Sue Nicholls** for the use of 'Mask Magic' © 1998, Sue Nicholls, previously unpublished; **Annette Penny** for the use of 'Sunday Boots and Working Boots' from *Super Stories for the Very Young* © 1989, Annette Penny (1989, Kingfisher); **Anne Piper** for 'Five Royal Knights' © 1998, Anne Piper, previously unpublished; **Jan Pollard** for the use of 'Old Clothes' © 1998, Jan Pollard, previously unpublished; **Lesley Prior** for the use of three assemblies © 1998, Lesley Prior, previously unpublished; **Maureen Warner** for the use of 'Let's Keep Out The Rain' © 1998, Maureen Warner, previously unpublished; **Stevie Ann Wilde** for the use of 'Special Clothes for Special People' © 1998, Stevie Ann Wilde, previously unpublished; **Brenda Williams** for the use of 'Shoes' and 'Getting Dressed' © 1998, Brenda Williams, previously unpublished.
Every effort has been made to trace copyright holders and the publishers apologise for any inadvertent omissions.

British Library Cataloguing-in-Publication Data A catalogue record for this book is available from the British Library.

ISBN 0-590-53720-2

The right of Anne Piper to be identified as the Author of this work has been asserted by her in accordance with the Copyright, Designs and Patents Act 1988.

All rights reserved. This book is sold subject to the condition that it shall not, by way of trade or otherwise, be lent, hired out or otherwise circulated without the publisher's prior consent in any form of binding or cover other than that in which it is published and without a similar condition, including this condition, being imposed upon the subsequent purchaser.

No part of this publication may be reproduced, stored in a retrieval system, or transmitted, in any form or by any means, electronic, mechanical, photocopying, recording or otherwise, without the prior permission of the publisher. This book remains copyright, although permission is granted to copy pages where indicated, for classroom distribution and use only in the school which has purchased the book, or by the teacher who has purchased this book and in accordance with the CLA licensing agreement. Photocopying permission is given for purchasers only and not for borrowers of books from any lending service.

CONTENTS

INTRODUCTION

Clothes have a special magic for children. Even the youngest child is likely to have a 'best outfit' or 'favourite colour' that they like to wear. From early on, children relish the chance to dress up on any occasion and are never far away from the dressing-up box! When you add to this the fact that clothes come in a myriad of shapes, colours and sizes, you can be confident that your topic will capture the children's enthusiasm from the start.

A theme on 'clothes' provides an all-encompassing range of topics for early years' practitioners. It offers rich opportunities to introduce young children, whether at home, in playgroup, nursery or reception class, to a range of basic concepts in stimulating ways which draw on their own experiences.

Throughout this book the emphasis is on encouraging children's observation and language skills. Through such an approach, young children can make their own 'connections' between different areas of the curriculum, relating their developing knowledge with personal experiences in their own lives.

LOOKING AT CLOTHES

Each chapter of the book looks at a different aspect of clothes. Chapter 1 concentrates on the children's own experiences of clothes, from getting dressed to going shopping for clothes. It looks at how their clothes' size has changed since they were babies, and focuses on 'decorative' dressing with jewellery. It provides the chance to set up a role-play shop, make button collages and investigate the best conditions for drying clothes. Chapter 2 helps children to understand that we need different types of clothing for different weather conditions. They learn that clothes can keep us warm and dry in winter, cool in summer and more visible in foggy conditions. They are encouraged to carry out simple science investigations, painting and sorting activities and have the chance to dress a 'weather teddy'. Chapter 3 provides a wider view by looking at a variety of special clothes, from the full regalia worn by a queen to costumes for clowns. It takes a look at clothes for special occasions, such as weddings and explores how clothes can function as uniforms and give us protection. Chapter 4 introduces clothes from other times and places, introducing a sense of 'what people used to wear' through works of art, posters, stories and artefacts. It also raises children's awareness of clothes in other parts of the world, offering a rich multicultural dimension with activities focusing on saris, kimonos, tartan and Welsh hats. Chapter 5 focuses on shoes and socks, starting from 'our feet' and moving on to look at different types of footwear, fastenings, colours, sizes, pairs and patterns. There are opportunities for drama and role-play through setting up a shoe shop and playing with 'sock puppets' made by the children themselves. Chapter 6 unravels the mystery for children of how clothes are made. It takes a look at raw materials and explores dyeing, pattern making, designs, materials and the purpose of labelling on clothes.

HOW TO USE THIS BOOK

Early years practitioners are faced with the constant challenge of introducing new learning experiences to children. These experiences need to be relevant and motivating for the children and practical for the adults to organise.

Young children learn best by actively doing things. Their understanding will be developed through practical experiences such as using sand, water and clay, utilising role-play areas and visiting interesting places. Activities must be pitched at a suitable level for the children's understanding, encouraging the development of speaking and listening skills which are vital to all areas of a young child's learning.

This book provides a collection of activity ideas on the theme of clothes, suitable for using with three- to six-years-old, either at home, in playgroups, nurseries, nursery classes or schools. The suggestions can be used and expanded on as part of the topic work being undertaken.

TOPIC WEB

This is a practical way of seeing how the clothes theme covers the preparation of all the subjects within the National Curriculum (Maths, English, Science, Design and Technology, Music, Art, Physical Education, Geography and History), as well as Religious Education and the subjects within the Scottish 5–14 Guidelines. The topic web can be photocopied and used as a checklist for your planning.

ACTIVITY PAGES

There are six chapters in this book, each covering a different aspect of clothes. Each chapter has eight activity pages which follow the same format, focusing on one main 'clothes' activity and including 'objectives' which prepare for a National Curriculum/Scottish Guidelines subject.

The 'group size' which is indicated is merely a suggestion and can obviously vary according to your premises, time and the adult to child ratio. 'Preparation' for activities has been kept to a minimum and you may find that the children themselves are able to help with this. This could involve making or setting out equipment. Alternatively, the children may need prior experience or knowledge which is essential to the success of the activity.

'What you need' sections are in the form of a simple list. If you are short of any item, it may well spoil the end result so it is advisable to gather everything before you start. The children will enjoy helping to collect items from home or within

your group. If the children know what they are going to be doing, it stimulates their interest and initiates keen anticipation.

'What to do' and the 'Discussion' sections are interdependent and it is not intended that these two sections should be dealt with separately. You will often be talking about what you are doing and questioning the children while they are completing the activity.

The 'Follow-up activities' are extensions of the same activity, or cross-curricula ideas for further work relating to the activity. They can be done at any time and may fit in with other activity pages.

The activities have been grouped in chapters but can be done in any order. This book should be used in the way that is most enjoyable and convenient for you and your group of children. Be open to the children's suggestions, share in their experiences and they will reward you with originality and true self-expression.

DISPLAYS

Some hints and ideas for displaying the children's work successfully are provided in this section. Three specific display suggestions are included, which draw on the work from different 'clothes' activity pages. Displays are a good way of instilling group co-operation and of recording children's work for you and for them. It is worth taking care in planning and labelling displays so that they can be used by everyone for observation, talking about, reading and enjoying.

ASSEMBLIES

The suggestions for assemblies and group sharing times all involve contributions from the children themselves. The ideas offer the chance to build on a rich multifaith and multicultural dimension within your topic.

RESOURCES

This includes stories, action rhymes, poems and songs based on the theme of clothes. Some link in closely with the activity suggestions and others offer a more general resource within the topic. The selection should provide a convenient and useful starting point. Much of this material has been commissioned to suit the topic and all the pages in this section can be photocopied.

PHOTOCOPIABLE ACTIVITY SHEETS

Eight photocopiable sheets are provided which all relate to specific activities in the book. Some photocopiable sheets will be more useful if enlarged to A3 size, as small children often find it easier to work on a larger scale. Adult help will be needed for younger children to complete their worksheets.

RECOMMENDED MATERIALS

This section refers to information and resource books, some of which have been used throughout this book. It also lists additional poetry and stories which would make a useful contribution to the theme of clothes.

THEMES
for early years

EXPRESSIVE ARTS

Planning towards the National Curriculum and the Scottish National guidelines 5-14

PHOTOCOPIABLE

PREPARING FOR PRIMARY SCHOOL

Children in the early years learn through first hand experiences, notably through play. They need to have opportunities to try out different skills and to learn concepts as they approach the requirements of the National Curriculum.

The National Curriculum was established to standardise the subjects, and the subject content, taught at all levels of a child's education. The intention is that any child will be able to go to school anywhere in the country and find the same areas of the curriculum being covered. These subjects are: English, Mathematics, Science, History, Geography, Design and Technology, Information Technology, PE, Art, Music and RE.

The activities suggested in this book cover all areas of the curriculum. Many are directed at small groups working together, but could equally be used with pairs of children or for children working alone. All children learn at different rates and have different paces of development so will need to be viewed by you, very much as individuals.

TOWARDS LEVEL ONE

The National Curriculum programmes of study apply to children who have reached the age of five. They were written to suit the abilities of children

who have reached their fifth birthday and have spent anything from a term to a year (depending on the part of the country in which they live) in a reception class. The National Curriculum provides an overall programme of study for each subject and requires teachers to assess the level of attainment of each child at the end of the key stage. The assessment is carried out partly through nationwide testing, but for the most part, it is left to the teacher's professional judgement to allocate an overall level to each child.

Before this time, children will be working towards its requirements under the provisions of the School Curriculum and Assessment Authority's Desirable Outcomes. The skills they will need include communication, observation, social and physical skills. These are not acquired through chance but through the provision of a carefully planned selection of activities. The ideas in this book allow for these vital skills to be developed through first hand experience.

THE SCOTTISH GUIDELINES 5–14

In Scotland there are National Guidelines for schools on what should be taught to children between the ages of five and fourteen. These are divided into six main areas: English Language, Mathematics, Environmental Studies, Expressive Arts, Religious and Moral Education and lastly Personal and Social Development. Within these main areas, further subjects are found, for example within Expressive Arts there is art and design, drama, music and PE.

Most nurseries will find that the experiences they are offering children will provide a good foundation for this curriculum. The activities in this book have been specifically written to prepare for many aspects of it, and will also fit well into the pre-five guidelines issued by the local authorities throughout Scotland.

The activities centred around the themes are shown in separate areas of the curriculum on the topic web (pages 8–9) to help with planning. The children's personal and social development is an ongoing theme and is incorporated throughout the activities outlined in this book.

CHAPTER 1
ME AND MY CLOTHES

In this chapter children learn how to dress in the right sequence and explore how their clothing needs change as they grow. They can find out how to make simple jewellery, create button collages, set up a clothes shop and even hold their own wash day!

GETTING DRESSED

Objective

English – To encourage sequencing and speaking and listening skills.

Group size

Up to six children.

What you need

The story *How do I put it on?* by Shigeo Watanabe (Red Fox) or any simple book about dressing, a baby-sized doll and a set of clothes to fit, including pants, a vest, socks, shorts and a jumper (try to include some with simple fasteners), one copy of photocopiable pages 88 and 89 (enlarged to A3) per pair of children, scissors, glue, pencils, crayons.

Preparation

How do I put it on? is a humorous story about a bear who puts his clothes on in all the wrong places, including putting his pants on his head! Read the story to the children, asking them where they think the bear will put each item of clothing before you turn the page to find out. Encourage them to share their own experiences in getting dressed with the group.

What to do

Let the children look at the baby-sized doll and the articles of clothing. Now ask the children to tell you how to dress the doll: What goes on first? How do we put it on? What goes on next? Encourage the children to talk about the order of the sequence during this part of the activity. Then, in pairs, let the children take turns to dress the doll (very young children will need an adult's help). Give copies of both photocopiable sheets to the children and ask them to each cut out the clothes and doll outline. Explain that you now want them to stick the clothes on the doll shape in the right order. Let them glue on the pants, vest and socks firmly, but show them how to stick the jumper and shorts by the top edge only, so that they can be lifted up like flaps. Let the children colour in the clothes and doll shapes, then encourage them to look at each other's dolls. Can they guess what colours the vest and pants underneath are before lifting up the clothes on top?

Discussion

Which clothes do you like to wear and why? Which clothes are the easiest to put on? Which ones are the most difficult? Does someone help you to get dressed in the morning? What clothes can you put on all by yourself?

Follow-up activities

✧ Make a collection of fasteners, including zips, buttons, Velcro, poppers, hooks and buckles. Talk about how these are used to fasten clothes.
✧ Sing 'Hooray for clothes' on page 80, and learn the action rhyme 'Getting dressed' on page 67.
✧ Read aloud the poem 'Clumsy giant gets up' on page 68 and learn the poem 'Picking up the clothes' by Sue Cowling on page 68.

GROWING

••••••••••••••••••••••••••••••••••

Objective

Science – To raise children's awareness of their own growth and development from babyhood to their present age.

Group size

Up to four children.

What you need

A collection of photographs of the children and members of staff as babies, a picture of a mother and baby (optional), a collection of clothes suitable for a baby, some clothes suitable for a five-year-old child, paper (A2 and A3), catalogues with pictures of baby equipment, pencils, ready-mixed paints, scissors.

Preparation

Look at the photographs of the children as babies and compare them with the children as they are now. Draw their attention to how their bodies have changed, such as the growth of hair and teeth, the

progress from crawling to standing and their increasing ability to use their hands. If possible, invite a mother to come in and bath her baby for the children. Talk about why we need to do things for babies and why we must handle them very gently.

What to do

Ask the children to draw or paint a picture of themselves as a baby. Cut out the pictures and mount them onto A3 paper. Draw a frame around the pictures and decorate it with 'things babies need', either drawn by the children or cut out from catalogues. Take an item of baby's clothing and a jumper or sweatshirt suitable for a five-year-old child. Lay these flat on a sheet of large paper and help the children to draw round them to get a basic shape (an adult will need to draw the outlines for younger children). While doing this, talk about the sizes of the clothes – which is the larger/smaller? The children can then paint their own designs onto the shapes and cut them out when dry.

Discussion

Talk about when the children were babies. What can they remember? Who looked after them? How did they eat? Where did they sleep? How did they get to places? Could they talk? Are all these things different now that they are bigger?

Follow-up activities

✧ Read *So Much* by T Cooke and H Oxenbury (Walker Books), *Peepo!* by Janet and Allan Ahlberg (Penguin) and *Bye Bye Baby* by Janet and Allan Ahlberg (Little Mammoth).

✧ Use poems about clothes to reinforce the idea of how we grow and change. Read to the children the poems 'Grown out of' by Tony Mitton on page 68, 'Second best' by Ian Larmont on page 67 and 'Old clothes' by Jan Pollard on page 71.

✧ Make a height chart. Compare the different heights and use the activity to reinforce vocabulary such as 'bigger than', 'smaller than', 'the same as'.

✧ Look at books which show different life cycles and discuss how baby animals change. Read *The Very Hungry Caterpillar* by Eric Carle (Penguin). Ask the children to draw pictures showing the different events in the story. Can they help you to put them in the correct sequence?

DECORATION

Objective

Design and Technology – To make a simple badge and necklace.

Group size

Up to six children.

What you need

Card, felt-tipped pens, a laminator or some sticky-backed plastic, sticky tape, safety-pins, buff school clay, clay tools or found materials, thin dowel, ready-mixed paints in bright colours, PVA glue, thin ribbon for threading.

Preparation

Cut the card into simple shapes such as circles, squares and triangles, measuring approximately 8cm × 8cm. Wear some interesting jewellery and bring the children's attention to it. Collect simple items of jewellery and look at pictures of people wearing jewellery.

What to do

Tell the children that they are going to make some badges. Ask them to choose a card shape and to draw the first letter of their name with a felt-tipped pen. Encourage them to decorate the badges using their own designs. Laminate the badges or cover with sticky-backed plastic and tape a safety-pin to the back so that the children can wear them.

Now move on to make some necklaces. Provide some clay and encourage the children to roll it in their hands to make several small balls (the size of mini tomatoes). Alternatively, they could shape the clay into squares, triangles or tubes. Let them draw textures and patterns onto the beads using clay tools or found materials. Push the beads onto thin dowel or a plastic straw to make a hole for threading. When the beads are leather hard, pull them off gently (this is best done by an adult). Allow the beads to dry completely. If a kiln is available, biscuit fire the beads, or simply leave them to harden, although they will not be as tough as fired beads. Decorate with ready-mixed paint.. You could use fluorescent paint which works well in this situation. Provide an equal mixture of PVA glue and water for the children to paint on the beads to produce a shiny finish. Thread the beads onto narrow ribbons and hold a parade so that each child can show his or her necklace off to the rest of the group.

Discussion

Talk about the jewellery collection. Why do we like to wear jewellery? What jewellery do we have for special times such as weddings? What is jewellery made of? What are your favourite kinds of jewellery? Have you ever visited a jewellery shop?

Follow-up activities

✧ Use beads for repeat pattern making, counting and matching according to colour, shape and size.
✧ Make a jewellery box. Ask the children to draw brightly coloured 'precious stones' in different shapes and stick these on to decorate the outside of a small cardboard box covered in silver or gold coloured foil.
✧ Write a story about hidden treasure. Think about who the treasure belonged to, how it got where it is now and how it was discovered. Scribe the story for the children if necessary and ask the children to draw pictures to illustrate the events.
✧ Sing 'Sparkling jewels for sale' on page 81.

SET UP SHOP

Objective

Drama – To encourage language development and to provide some experience in handling money through role-play.

Group size

Up to six children.

What you need

New Clothes for Alex by Mary Dickinson and Charlotte Firmin (Hippo Books), a collection of dressing-up clothes (hats are especially useful), a role-play screen (to section off the 'shop' area), a till and some money (preferably real), small containers or purses, shopping bags, hangers or a small clothes rack to display clothes, labels (for prices), large sheets of paper, car sponge (or similar) and paint (for printing), paper, felt-tipped pens, a laminator or some sticky-backed plastic.

Preparation

Read the children the story *New Clothes for Alex*. Talk about the children's own experiences of shopping for clothes. Then explain that they are going to help you set up a clothes shop in your room. Brainstorm the things you will need. Mark off the 'shop' area with the role-play screen. Provide a car sponge or similar and some red paint, and show the children how to print onto large

sheets of paper to create a brick-effect. Fix the paper onto the outside walls of your shop. Set up a chair and table inside the 'shop' with a till containing change. Provide some receipts and a pencil. Fill six small containers or purses with coins up to a total of 20p. For younger children use 1p and 2p coins only and for older children supply 1p, 2p, 5p and 10p coins.

What to do

Ask the children to create posters advertising what your shop has for sale. Invent names for goods such as 'jazzy jumpers', 'super socks', 'bouncy boots'. Provide the children with brightly coloured paints or thick felt-tipped pens to decorate the posters. Make an 'open/closed' sign and price labels to pin or tape to the clothes. Keep the prices to a maximum of 10p. Laminate the price tags and posters or cover with sticky-backed plastic to make them last longer.

Now the children are ready to shop. Start off by suggesting that the group are buying new clothes to go to a wedding or a party, then let them come up with their own ideas. Supervise them in the role-play area to encourage discussion about money and to help them recognise different coins and their values.

Discussion

How do you choose your clothes? What colours do you like to wear? What types of shops have you visited? What do they sell? What is your favourite shop? What does it sell? How do you get there? How are supermarkets different to smaller shops?

Follow-up activities

✧ Set up shops based around characters from stories or fairy tales, such as Cinderella's shoe shop (see Chapter 5, page 44), The Mad Hatter's hat shop, The Hungry Caterpillar's fruit shop.
✧ Ask the children to bring in different carrier bags and put a collection on display. Let them use this as a stimulus to design their own shop logo and handle suitable for a carrier bag.

BUTTONS

Objective

Art – To make a collage picture using buttons.

Group size

Up to six children.

What you need

A collection of buttons with as much variety in shape, colour, size and texture as possible, thin card (A4), thick and thin felt-tipped pens or brightly coloured pencil crayons, PVA glue.

Preparation

Encourage the children to collect some buttons. Set up a table with labels asking the children to sort the buttons by size, shape, colour, number of holes and material. After some experience with the 'button table', tell the children that they are going to make pictures using buttons.

What to do

Look at the buttons with the children. Ask them to choose six of their favourite ones. What picture could they make with these buttons? Could it be a wheel, or perhaps an eye or a nose? Encourage more suggestions from the children. Show them how to stick their buttons onto card using glue and make up a picture around them using felt-tipped pens or crayons. Use the pictures to create a colourful wall display.

Discussion

What are buttons for? Which children can do up their buttons? Which buttons are the hardest to do up? Which clothes usually have buttons? How many different things can the children say about a button? Is it big or small? What colour is it? How many holes does it have? Is the button on their shirt or coat? What does it help them to fasten up?

Follow-up activities

◇ Use buttons to make jewellery. Thread them onto strong cotton to create simple bracelets and necklaces, or stick them firmly onto different card shapes to make badges.

◇ Make simple 'button shakers'. Sort the buttons into some large plastic pots (yoghurt pots work well) according to their size and material. Secure the lids tightly before shaking. How many different sounds do the pots make? Which buttons make the loudest noise? Which ones make the least noise?

FRIENDSHIP BRACELETS

Objective

RE – To make a friendship bracelet and give it to a friend.

Group size

Up to six children.

What to do

Measure each child's wrist and cut a strip of card to the correct size. Use the hole punch to make a row of holes about 2cm apart along the length of the card. (Adult help will be needed for this.) Choose two colours of ribbon and cut into lengths at least 12cm longer than the card strips. Show the children how to thread the ribbon in and out of the holes, alternating the colours. When the threading is finished, knot the ribbon at each end

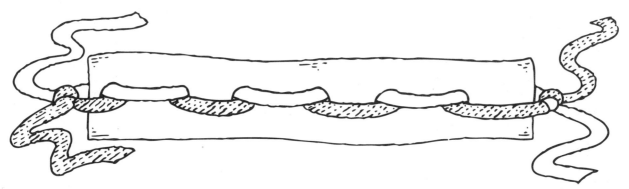

What you need

Thin card (for making bracelets), a single hole punch, thin ribbon in different colours.

Preparation

Talk to the children about having friends. How do they recognise a friend when they are with lots of other children? What do their friends look like? Are they all the same or different? How do you show that you are someone's friend? What kinds of things do friends do for each other? Explain to the children that they are now going to make a friendship bracelet to give to a friend.

to stop it pulling back through. The bracelets are now ready for the children to each give to a friend for them to wear.

Discussion

Why do we give presents to our friends? Is it to show that we like them? Is it to make them feel good? Is it to make ourselves feel good? In what other ways can we show how important our friends are to us? What special occasions do we like to celebrate by giving presents? What kind of presents do the children like to receive?

Follow up activities

✧ Read *Aldo* by John Burningham (Red Fox), a story about an imaginary friend called Rabbit. This is a useful book for stimulating discussion on loneliness and bullying.
✧ Look at some of the Bible stories which describe how Jesus helped people and/or read the story of the Good Samaritan. Use it as a basis for talking about being kind to other people. What things do the children do to help their friends or family? Do they enjoy helping other people?
✧ Make a surprise box for a friend with a message inside. Decorate a small cardboard box by covering with strips of tissue paper and collage materials. Write a message to your friend or your parents and hide it in the box.

LET'S DO THE WASHING!

Objective

History – To compare a piece of Victorian laundry equipment with its modern day equivalent.

Group size

Up to six children.

What you need

Some pieces of equipment used in a Victorian laundry such as a flat iron, a washboard, dolly pegs, a large block of green soap (try ironmongers or market stalls), a large wooden scrubbing brush, pictures of modern washing equipment including a washing machine, tumble dryer and electric iron, posters of old adverts such as Pears Soap (see page 96), the story *Mrs Lather's Laundry* by Allan Ahlberg (Penguin), paper, pencils.

Preparation

Write to parents and grandparents asking for help with this activity as Victorian kitchen equipment is widely used for ornaments around the home. Alternatively, contact your local museum who may loan you some artefacts.

Prepare the children by reading them *Mrs Lather's Laundry*. The family in this story run an old-fashioned laundry, but become bored with washing clothes and so decide to wash babies, dogs and elephants! Talk about the laundry equipment used in the story and put your collection of artefacts on display. Discuss the display with the children, explaining that it will help them to find out how people washed their clothes a long time ago in Victorian times.

What to do

Look at the flat iron and the modern electric iron. Ask the children what the modern iron is for. How does it work? What makes it become hot? Now ask them what they think the flat iron is. How do they think it was used? How did it become hot? What happened when it got cold? Look at the materials that the irons are made of, such as plastic and metal for the modern iron, cast iron for the flat iron. Encourage the children to do an observational drawing of the irons to help them make comparisons. Show individual children's drawings to the rest of the group and note the differences which the children have observed.

Discussion

How is the children's washing done? Have they been to a launderette? Who does their washing and ironing? Why should we be very careful about touching irons? When is it not safe to touch them?

Follow-up activities

✧ Make some simple 'marbling-effect' paintings. Dip sheets of cartridge paper into the water and shake off any excess drops. Drip some paint onto the wet paper to create patterns. Leave flat to dry.
✧ Read *The Tale of Mrs Tiggy Winkle* by Beatrix Potter (World International).
✧ Sing 'Rub-a-dub-a-dub' on page 82.
✧ Learn the poems 'How did your mum do the washing, Gran?' on page 69 and 'Burger bar girl' on page 71.

BUBBLES

Objective

Science — To find the best drying conditions for washed fabric samples.

Group size

Up to six children.

What you need

An old cotton sheet or pre-washed cotton fabric, a water-play tray or washing-up bowl, washing-up liquid, string to make a washing line, pegs, paper, pencils, crayons, glue sticks, scissors.

Preparation

Choose a breezy sunny day. Tell the children that you want to wash all the dolls' clothes because they are dirty, but first you need to find the best place for drying washing. Set up the water tray or washing-up bowl with warm soapy water and cut up the cotton sheet or pre-washed fabric into 12 squares. Explain to the children that they are going to wash the fabric and hang it in different places to find the best conditions for drying clothes.

What to do

Allow the children to wash the cotton pieces in the warm soapy water and show them how to wring out the excess water. Suggest that they hang the washing in four different places: outside in a sunny spot and in a shady spot; inside, with the fabric hung on the line away from the window; inside, with the fabric placed on a flat surface.

Set up the washing lines and hang out the washing using the pegs (some young children will need an adult's help). Encourage the children to decide when they are going to check the washing to see if it is dry. They can record their findings using a cut-and-stick record sheet.

Discussion

Encourage the children to explain why some of the washing has dried and some has not. Talk about what is needed to help clothes dry. Why do we have washing lines that move around? Why do tumble dryers blow air and move the clothes around a lot? Bring in the following vocabulary: soak, wash, wring, squeeze, dry and damp.

Follow-up activities

✧ Read *Doing the Washing* by Sarah Garland (Puffin).
✧ Look through shop catalogues and magazines to find pictures of washing lines and washing equipment.
✧ Blow bubbles and look at the colours in them. Write a poem describing what bubbles look like, or invent a story about a bubble that floats away to a magical place.
✧ Learn the poem 'Pssst!' on page 72.

CHAPTER 2
CLOTHES AND THE WEATHER

Activities in this chapter will help the children to understand why we need different clothes for different weather conditions. There are ideas for carrying out simple testing of materials and recording the daily weather, as well as art and drama activities.

WILL IT KEEP ME DRY?

Objective

Science – To find out which fabrics are waterproof.

Group size

Up to six children.

What you need

The children's coats, six large identical yoghurt pots, six thick elastic bands, six fabric samples including knitted wool, cotton, nylon, PVC, silk and felt, six droppers, water.

Preparation

Choose a rainy day as this will make the activity more relevant for the children. Ask them what clothes they wear to keep dry. Ask them to put on their coats and take them out in the rain for a short time. Back inside, look at each child's coat and feel the materials they are made from. Then show the children the six fabric samples and talk about what they are made from. Now tell them that you want them to find out which fabric sample would be best to make a rain coat from.

What to do

Show the children how to stretch each fabric sample across the top of a yoghurt pot and fix tightly with elastic bands. Fill the droppers with equal amounts of water. Squeeze one dropper onto each fabric sample. Look carefully at what happens to the water.

Discussion

Did the water run off any of the fabric? Was it easy to make the water go through the fabric? Which material would the children use to make a coat that would keep them dry? Bring in the vocabulary: absorbent, non-absorbent, waterproof, saturated.

Follow-up activities

✧ Draw some large raindrops on white paper and cut them out. Hold a brainstorming session and encourage the children to think of as many 'rainy day' words as they can. Examples could include: raindrop, splash, trickle, drizzle, pour, shower, thunder, storm, rain. Write these words on the raindrops and display them around the room so they can be clearly seen.

✧ Teach the children some traditional rhymes about rain, including 'Rain, rain, go away', 'Incy Wincy Spider', and 'It's raining, it's pouring'.

✧ Record the rainy days for one month. Make a chart showing the number of wet days and dry days for that month.

✧ Read 'Happiness' by A A Milne from *When We Were Very Young* (Mammoth).

✧ Think of well-known expressions about rain, such as 'raining cats and dogs' and 'bucketing down'. Encourage the children to paint amusing pictures to illustrate the sayings.

✧ Say the rhyme 'Let's keep out the rain' on page 70, and sing 'Me and my clothes' on page 82.

A SUNNY DAY

Objective

Art — To look at a famous work of art from the past and compare the clothes it illustrates with present day fashion.

Group size

Up to six children.

What you need

A print of *Sunday Afternoon on the Isle of Grand Jatte* by George Pierre Seurat (1859-91) from a book of his work, viewfinders (small card frames to help focus on a specific part of the painting), thick, brightly coloured paint for finger painting, paper (A3 and A4), fine black pens.

Preparation

Show the children the Seurat picture. Explain that the Isle of Grand Jatte is near to Paris and was a place where people liked to go on their days off. Encourage the children to look carefully at the clothes the people are wearing in the picture. Are the clothes different from the ones we wear today? Look for interesting details in the picture. Turn this into an 'I Spy' game, for example: 'I spy a fan on the ground', 'I spy a pet monkey', 'I spy a soldier', 'I spy a lady fishing'. Ask the children to look at the shape of the women's dresses. How do they think the skirts were made to look so wide? Tell them that bustles were cane frameworks which were worn under skirts to give them a fuller shape.

Help the children to notice how Seurat painted his picture using hundreds of tiny dots (a technique called *pointillism*). Ask them to look for dark and light areas on the painting. How did Seurat achieve this effect?

What to do

Give each child a viewfinder and ask them to choose a small part of the painting to copy in detail. Provide them with fine black pens and some A4 paper. Explain that you want them to use line only and not to shade or 'colour in' their pictures. Photocopy the finished drawings at 141% onto A3 paper. The children can now paint these enlarged versions. Show them how to use a finger dipped in thick paint to create lots of small dots to fill in each section of their picture. Mount and display the children's paintings together with their original smaller drawings and the Seurat print. (See page 63 for ideas on creating a full display based around the Seurat picture.)

Discussion

Tell the children that the real Seurat painting is very large, measuring 2m × 3m. Show them how large this is by comparing it with the size of a wall in your room. How long do they think it took Seurat to paint the picture? (It took him two years.) Explain that Seurat did not work from just one large scene, but used ideas from lots of smaller drawings he made to help him build up the detail. Do the children like the design of the painting? How would they arrange the figures? Do the clothes in the painting look comfortable? What would we wear today in the park on a sunny day?

Follow-up activities

✧ Make a second enlarged copy of the children's drawings and ask them to arrange these onto a large background to make their own 'work of art'.
✧ Help the children create an adventure story about a sunny day in the park. Encourage them to describe the scene in as much detail as possible. Who do they go to the park with? What happens when they get there? What do they eat if they take a picnic? Scribe the story in a book and stick in children's pictures to illustrate the story.
✧ Collect pictures from magazines and catalogues to make a collage of clothes for a sunny day.

BRR, I FEEL COLD!

Objective

Drama – To make a 'cold place' for the role-play area.

Group size

Up to six children.

What you need

Three or more white cotton sheets, a screen (optional), white crêpe paper, strips of silver paper, white cartridge paper, pictures and posters of cold scenes including some in other countries, books and puzzles about winter and Arctic regions, woolly hats, scarves, gloves, chalk or crayons in 'cold' colours (white, blue, grey), blue sugar paper, scissors, a small table, two chairs.

Preparation

Talk about feeling cold in the winter. Tell the children about some cold places in the world, such as Iceland and the Arctic regions. Explain that in some places the winter is much colder and longer than in our country. Show them posters, books and puzzles about cold places. Ask them which colours they associate with the cold and why. How do they dress to keep warm on a cold winter's day?

What to do

Ask the children to help you make a 'cold place' in your room. A corner is the easiest space to use for this, especially if a screen is not available. Spread a white sheet on the floor and drape some white sheets on the wall with drawing pins or staples. Fold circles of white paper for the children to cut into snowflakes. Cut long strips of white crêpe paper and staple the snowflakes to the strips. Hang these from the ceiling. Cut icicle shapes from silver paper and hang all around the inside of the role-play area. Put some hats, scarves and gloves in a box outside the 'cold place'. Set up a small table and two chairs inside the area with books and puzzles about winter or cold places. Set up some

drawing activities, providing chalk or crayons in 'cold' colours and some blue or grey paper. Finally, explain to the children that this is a very cold place and they will need to wear warm clothes before they can play there.

Discussion

How does it feel to be in the cold place? Would you like to live in a very cold country? What do you know about cold countries? What kind of animals live there?

Follow-up activities

✧ Make a large wall collage of a cold place using torn paper in 'cold' colours. Include any plants or animals that might live there. Ask older children to find out some simple facts about cold places. Write these on cards and stick them around the collage.
✧ Read *Penguin Small* by Mick Inkpen (Hodder Children's Books).
✧ Watch *The Snowman* video based on the story by Raymond Briggs. Ask the children if they have ever made a snowman. Can they describe to the other children how they did it? What happened to their snowman when the weather became warmer?
✧ Find out about people who live in cold places, such as the Inuit Indians. How do these people keep warm? What kind of houses do they live in? How do they provide heat in these houses?
✧ Sing 'Clothes for a cold day' on page 83.

CAN YOU SEE MY CLOTHES?

Objective

Science – To test to find out whether dark or bright colours show up best in the fog and to make a fluorescent star badge.

Group size

Up to six children.

What you need

A box with a lid (approximately 32cm × 24cm), dark grey paper, thin card, bright fluorescent paper and card, dark paper, Blu-Tack, a laminator or some sticky-backed plastic, pencils, scissors, safety-pins, tape.

Preparation

Cut a peep-hole in one end of the box and line with dark grey paper. Cut two body shapes measuring 15cm tall from thin card. Make some clothes shapes to fit the bodies from bright fluorescent paper and dark paper. Prepare several star templates cut from card (for the badge-making activity).

What to do

Show the children some sheets of fluorescent paper and dark coloured paper. Ask them to sort the paper into a 'bright pile' and a 'dark pile'. Tell them that they are going to find out which colours would be easiest to see on a foggy day. Explain they will also have the chance to make a star badge to wear from the colour that shows up best.

Show the box and card body shapes to the children. Tell them that you are going to dress the body shapes in different colours and put these inside the box where it is very dark. The children are going to peep through the hole to find out which card shape is the easiest to see. (Give each body shape a name at this point, to make it easier for the children to talk about them.) Fix the fluorescent clothes on one body shape and the dark clothes on the other. Stick both shapes inside the box at the opposite end to the peep-hole. Let one child at a time peep through the hole to find out which colour shows up best.

Repeat the activity using several colour combinations.

Help the children to record their findings. When they have discovered that the bright colours are the easiest to see they are ready to make their star badge. Provide the star templates for them to draw around onto the fluorescent card and cut out (younger children will need help with this). Laminate the star shapes or cover with sticky-backed plastic and tape on safety-pins to finish the badges.

Discussion

Talk about road safety when out in the fog or dark. Why is it important to be seen? What do the children need to do when walking to school in the fog? What do cyclists or walkers do to make themselves more visible? Can the children think of other people who might wear fluorescent clothing as part of their job to make them more easily seen?

Follow-up activities

✧ Make a 'foggy day' picture by placing a sheet of white tissue over the children's drawings or paintings.
✧ Read *Postman Pat's Foggy Day* by John Cunliffe (Hippo Books).
✧ Design a string trail to help a walker find their way in the fog. Make clear signs and notices using large letters on bright backgrounds.

UMBRELLAS

Objective

Mathematics – To paint large umbrellas using repeat patterns.

Group size

Up to six children.

What you need

Paper (A3 or larger), ready-mixed paint in bright colours, large and small paint brushes, a collection of umbrellas.

Preparation

Draw several large 'open' umbrella shapes (one for each child) onto A3 paper and cut them out. Draw six equal sections on each shape. Now look at the umbrella collection with the children. Can they explain what we use umbrellas for? Have they got an umbrella? Are umbrellas difficult to use? Look at the different designs and sizes of the umbrellas and talk about the colours and patterns on them.

What to do

Give each child one of the paper umbrellas shapes. Explain that they are going to paint a pattern in each of the first three sections of the umbrella and then copy this exactly into the second three sections (see diagram). Encourage them to use a variety of colours and patterns.

Discussion

Talk about how umbrellas protect us, keeping us and our clothes dry in the rain and giving us shade in the sun. Use simple pattern vocabulary: stripe, spot, zigzag, line, check, criss-cross. Talk about

repeating colour sequences and pattern sequences. Encourage younger children to repeat their pattern sequence verbally, such as 'red, blue, green, red, blue, green,' or 'spot, square, stripe, spot, square, stripe'.

Follow-up activities

✧ Create a 'rainy day' display. Write some 'rainy day' words on pieces of paper cut into raindrop shapes. Fix the children's finished umbrellas on the wall and place the 'raindrops' above them.

✧ Make some umbrella-shaped books with the children and encourage them to write 'rainy day' poems or stories inside with pictures to illustrate them.

✧ Look at Pierre-Auguste Renoir's painting *Les Parapluies* in a book of his work.

✧ Learn the poem 'Let's keep out the rain' on page 70.

BOOTS

Objective

Mathematics – To collect and sort wellington boots by colour and size, following up with photocopiable sheets at different levels.

Group size

Whole group.

What you need

A collection of wellington boots, a copy of photocopiable page 90 for each younger child, paper, a black writing pen (to make photocopiable sheets for older children), pencils and crayons.

Preparation

Collect boots in a variety of colours and sizes. Copy photocopiable page 90 for younger children. Make your own sheets for older children, drawing boots which the children have to count and add in twos as well as sort by size.

What to do

Look at the boot collection with the children. Why do we wear boots? What are boots made of? Ask them to help you sort the boot collection. Can they order the boots by size, starting from the smallest? Next, see if they can sort the boots by height, then by colour and finally by pattern on the soles. When the children have had plenty of experience in sorting the boots in different ways they can complete the photocopiable sheets. Give each younger child a copy of the photocopiable sheet on page 90. Give older children the worksheets you have prepared to give them practice in adding in twos and ordering by size.

Discussion

Do boots keep your feet dry? Are they made from waterproof materials? What size are your boots? Do they fit? Are they tight or loose? Who else might wear special boots? What happens to your feet in your boots on a wet day? What happens if your boots have a hole in?

Follow-up activities

✧ Use a large boot and fill it with objects beginning with 'b', such as a brush, a ball, a button and so on. Provide labels clearly marked with lowercase 'b' and with the names of each object. Use these with the children as part of a phonics session.
✧ Make a chart showing the children's boot sizes and boot colours.
✧ Read *New Boots for Alfie* by Shirley Hughes (Walker Books).

THE WEATHER TEDDY

Objective

Geography – To make and dress a 'weather teddy'.

What you need

Photocopiable pages 91 and 92 (to make the 'weather teddy' and his clothes), paper (A3), thin card, felt-tipped pens, crayons, scissors, a laminator or sticky-backed plastic.

Preparation

Photocopy the 'weather teddy' and his clothes onto A3 paper, increasing the size to 141%. Colour the teddy and his clothes. Mount the teddy onto card, cut out and laminate or cover with sticky-backed plastic. Cut out the clothes ready for the teddy to wear.

What to do

Show the children the 'weather teddy' and his clothes. Explain to them that he needs to be dressed in the right clothes for the weather that day. Talk about what the weather is like and ask the children to dress the bear in clothes they think are appropriate.

Show them how to fold the tabs over to hold the clothes onto the bear. (Tie tabs may need strengthening with sticky tape along the back.) To cover the different types of weather, tell the children that the bear is going on holiday to a place where it is either hot, cold or rainy.

Discussion

Talk to the children about the clothes we wear in different types of weather. Look at some examples of clothing for a variety of weather conditions. Encourage the children to sort the clothing into groups and give reasons for their decisions, such as, 'I put this on the rainy day pile because it is waterproof', 'I put this on the cold day pile because it is warm and woolly'.

Follow-up activities

✧ Let the children imagine that they are going on holiday to a hot place. Bring in a suitcase and a mixture of clothes for cold, hot and wet weather. Include other items like a towel, bathing costume, sun cream and so on. What will the children pack in their suitcase and what will they leave behind?

✧ Talk to the children about safety in the sun. How can they protect their skin and eyes? Ask them to help you create a 'safety in the sun' display. Make sun-hat and parasol shapes cut from paper. Make some sunglasses using card for the frames and cellophane for the lenses. Add some empty sun-tan lotion bottles and encourage older children to design 'safety in the sun' posters.

✧ Make a bag or suitcase to keep the 'weather teddy's' clothes in.

✧ Make a display showing different clothes for different weathers.

HOLD ON TO YOUR HAT!

Objective

Geography – To make 'wind bracelets' to find out which way the wind is blowing.

Group size

Up to six children.

What you need

A windy day, the story *The Wind Blew* by Pat Hutchins (Red Fox), card, tissue paper, sticky tape, paper, pencils, crayons.

Preparation

This activity should be carried out on a windy day. Prepare some thin card strips measuring approximately 2.5cm wide and long enough to fit around the children's wrists. Cut plenty of thin tissue paper strips measuring approximately 10cm long.

Read *The Wind Blew* to the children. This story is about a windy day; the wind blows various articles into the air such as a kite, a wig, some letters and scarves, and drops them back down onto the wrong people. The wind then blows out to sea. Encourage the children to look carefully at the illustrations to spot what will happen next. Talk about the illustrations. How can they tell from the pictures that it is a windy day? What is happening to the trees and the people's clothes? Can they remember all the things the wind blew away? What happens to them when they go out in the wind? Can they tell which way the wind is blowing?

What you do

Now the children can make some wind bracelets which will help them to see the way the wind is blowing. Measure each child's wrist with a strip of card, allowing a little extra for fixing. Stick the ends of the long tissue paper strips onto the card with sticky tape (adult help will be needed). Place the card around each child's wrist again and fix with sticky tape or staple it for them. Take the children outside and ask them to hold their hands in the air, looking carefully at the tissue paper strips. Can

they tell which way is the wind blowing? Talk about what happened to their wind bracelets. (You could introduce older children to the four main compass points.) Later, the children can draw pictures showing what they found out about the wind from the story and from feeling it on them during the wind bracelet activity.

Discussion

What does the wind feel like? Do you like to be out in the wind? What does the wind do to your clothes and hair? Is it best to wear loose or tight clothes in the wind? Does the wind make you feel cold? Are there any clothes which the wind cannot blow through?. Bring in appropriate vocabulary: blow, breeze, gale, strong, gusty, blustery, hurricane, tornado, windswept, windproof.

Follow-up activities

✧ Try doing some blow painting. Put a blob of runny paint on a piece of paper and blow through a straw or straight onto the paper. What happens to the paint?
✧ Read the story *Mrs Mopple's Washing Line* by Anita Hewett and Robert Broomfield (Red Fox).
✧ Read the poem 'Who has seen the wind?' by Christina Rossetti (Everyman Poetry).

CHAPTER 3
SPECIAL CLOTHES

Here children can look at the clothes people wear for doing specific jobs or activities. They can also find out about clothes we wear for special celebrations like weddings and make their own carnival masks. There is also the chance to have their faces painted like clowns!

KINGS AND QUEENS

Objective

Design and Technology — To design and make a crown.

Group size

Up to six children.

What you need

Posters and pictures in books showing Queen Elizabeth II in full regalia, a close-up picture of the Crown jewels, card, bright or fluorescent ready-mixed paints, crêpe paper, collage materials such as sequins, buttons, pasta and Cellophane (to decorate the 'crowns'), Marvin medium glue, a stapler, white paper (A4), pencils, scissors, masking tape.

Preparation

To prepare the main part of the crowns, cut some card into strips measuring approximately 20cm wide and 35cm long (one for each child). Cut crêpe paper into large circles, about the size of a round tea-tray (to fit inside the 'crowns').

Let the children look at pictures of the clothes Queen Elizabeth II wore at her Coronation and the clothes she dresses in for state occasions today. Focus on the crown — what shapes can they see? Do the shapes form a pattern?

What to do

Explain to the children that they are each going to make a crown to wear. Use the strips of card to measure their head size. Mark with a pencil and then cut leaving an overlap for joining. Encourage

older children to draw a picture of the crown they want to make, using some of the shapes they have seen in the pictures. Help them to draw on the shape they have chosen and cut it out. For younger children, provide a selection of ready-drawn shapes to choose from. These can be cut out by an adult after measuring the child's head size. The children can then paint their crowns with bright colours and leave them to dry.

Decorate the crowns by sticking on a range of collage materials with glue. When dry, bend the crowns round, then staple and fix them with masking tape along the edge. Use the circles of crêpe paper to represent velvet. Push the crêpe paper inside the crown, pleat it and staple to the crown (adult help will be needed with this). The crown is now finished and ready to wear.

Discussion

Why does the Queen needs to wear a crown and special clothes? What sort of clothes do you think she wears on ordinary days? Would you like to be king or queen? What sort of jobs might you have to do? What is Queen Elizabeth's crown made of?

Follow-up activities

◇ Make cloaks from old curtains to wear with the crowns and hold a royal parade.
◇ Turn the role-play area into a palace. Act out episodes from a typical day in the life of a king or queen.
◇ Sing 'There was a princess long ago' *This Little Puffin* (Penguin).

PEOPLE WHO HELP US

Objective

RE – To learn about people who help us.

Group size

Up to six children.

What you need

A work uniform (borrowed from a parent or a local business), paper (A4), black handwriting pens, photocopier, card, Plasticine in different colours, felt-tipped pens or good wax crayons.

Preparation

Show the children a work uniform. Who does it belong to? What is their job? Why do they wear a uniform? What is it made of? Brainstorm with the children a list of people who help us. Talk about the different roles of these people. What sort of clothes do they wear and why? Is it to protect them or help to keep them clean? Does it help us to identify them easily? Does it make them look smart?

Based on your list of people who help us, draw simple background pictures to provide a context, such as a front door for post and milk deliverers, a road for traffic police, a bed for a nurse or doctor, a dustbin for a refuse collector, a van with a cross on for an ambulance driver. Photocopy these for the children to choose from.

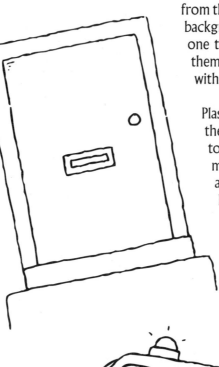

What to do

Ask the children to each choose one person from the list of people who help us. Provide the background pictures and ask each child to find one to match with their chosen person. Let them colour and fill in the background detail with felt-tipped pens.

Now ask the children to make a Plasticine model of that person to fit onto their background picture. Encourage them to add as much detail as possible to their model to help identify which person they are representing. When they have finished, let them place their model onto the pictures. They can then move the figure into different positions around their picture, perhaps acting out a story.

Discussion

Why do we need all these people to help us? What would happen if they weren't there? Encourage the children to relate their own experience of meeting one of these people.

Follow-up activities

✧ Invite a policeman or a nurse in to talk to the children about the work they do. Ask them to bring in their uniform to show the children.

✧ Turn the role-play area into a hospital or post office. Provide props to create as realistic an environment as possible. Let an adult supervise the children to help them develop the different scenarios.

✧ Read some *Postman Pat* stories by John Cunliffe (Hippo Books).

✧ Sing the song 'Uniforms' on page 85.

WAITERS AND WAITRESSES

Objective

Drama – To make a café in the role-play area.

Group size

Up to six children.

What you need

The story of *Mrs Wobble the Waitress* by Allan Ahlberg (Penguin), a screen (to section off the 'café' area), two small tables, five chairs, a table cloth, four sets of cutlery, four cups, plates and dishes, Plasticine, paper flowers in a pot (to decorate the 'customer's' table), a box of dressing up clothes (for the 'café customers'), white crêpe paper, stapler, card, large paper-clips, felt-tipped pens, a laminator or some sticky-backed plastic, four purses each filled with a variety of coins to a total of 20p, a till, a small note pad (for orders and receipts).

Preparation

Read the story of *Mrs Wobble the Waitress* to the children. Mrs Wobble is a waitress who loses her job because she wobbles and drops jelly on the manager's head. The Wobble family then decide to open a café of their own. Mrs Wobble becomes famous for her wobbling. Let the children look at the pictures in the book to see the clothes that the Wobble family wear to work in their café. Why do they need these special clothes? Is it to make them look smart? Is it to help keep them clean? Do these clothes help customers to recognise them?

Prepare the children by visiting a real café if possible, or show them some pictures. Explain that they are going to set up their own café in your room. Can they tell you what things they will need?

What to do

Section off a small area of your room using a screen if available. Provide a table and four chairs for the 'customers'. Place a till on another small table and provide a chair for the 'manager'. Ask the children what type of food their café will sell. Help them to make simple items of food such as buns and cakes

using Plasticine or card shapes coloured in. Create posters for the café advertising the food on sale. Make menus with prices up to 10p (laminate or cover with sticky-backed plastic). Create simple hats and aprons for the waiter/waitress and manager by stapling white crêpe paper to thin bands of card. Fasten them with large paper-clips.

Let the children set the table using the table-cloth, flowers, cups, plates and cutlery. Provide each 'customer' with the dressing-up clothes and purses filled with coins. The children are now ready to declare their café open!

Discussion

Have you ever visited a café? What was it like? Can you remember what the waiters or waitresses wore? How would you feel if a waiter/waitress looked dirty or untidy? Why is it important to keep clean when handling food? Why should you wear an apron and wash your hands before you begin to cook?

Follow-up activities

✧ Make some salt dough food to serve in your café. Use different food colouring for variety.
✧ Draw some cup-shapes on card or paper and cut them out. Write on each one a word linked with a café, such as 'tea', 'cup', 'plate' and so on, using large letters. Hang these around your café so that the children can see them clearly.
✧ Make cakes or sandwiches to serve in your café.

LET'S GET MARRIED!

Objective

English – To learn and play the traditional singing game 'Poor Jenny sits a-weeping'.

Group size

Whole group

What you need

A collection of wedding clothes, including a wedding dress if possible, the song 'Poor Jenny sits a-weeping' on page 84, some dressing-up hats such as a bride's veil, a groom's top hat, hats for bridesmaids, page boys and a parson.

Preparation

Collect some wedding clothes and photographs, including old pictures if possible. Look at the collection with the children and introduce some basic vocabulary: veil, train, gown, bouquet, top hat, tails, head-dress, tiara. Look carefully at the fabrics used in the wedding clothes and how traditional dresses for brides and bridesmaids are decorated. Explain to the children that there are lots of different types of weddings, and that they can be held in many other places apart from churches. Draw on the children's experiences about any weddings they have attended and the clothes they wore on these occasions. (Any discussion about weddings will need sensitive handling.)

What to do

Teach the children the song 'Poor Jenny sits a-weeping'. Then ask them to form a circle. Choose one child as 'Jenny' to sit in the middle. (You can adapt the words to 'Poor Johnny' to start the game with a boy.) The other children should then dance round her while they sing. (Try changing direction in different verses, as this will add to the fun!) 'Jenny' must choose other children to join her in the middle of the circle in verses three to seven. (Use the dressing-up hats to represent the different characters.) At the end of the eighth verse, all the children form a procession led by the parson, followed by 'Jenny' and her retinue.

Discussion

Talk about how weddings are celebrated in different communities or other countries. What sort of food are guests given? How long do the celebrations last? Talk about popular customs and traditions associated with weddings such as wedding cakes, honeymoons, the bride throwing the bouquet. Have the children heard the traditional rhyme 'something old, something new, something borrowed, something blue'? What do they think it means?

Follow-up activities

✧ Listen to the wedding march by Felix Mendelssohn.
✧ Make some wedding invitations from card and decorate them with simple drawings of bells, flowers and so on.
✧ Find out about good luck symbols. What things do we consider to be lucky? Let the children draw pictures of horseshoes, black cats, wishing wells and four-leaf clovers to display in a 'lucky corner' of the room.
✧ Make a large collage picture of a bride and groom. Decorate the picture with an archway of tissue paper flowers.

HARD HATS

Objective

Art – To make mono-print swirls for creating snail shell 'hard hats'.

Group size

Up to six children.

What you need

A collection of helmets and hard hats (borrowed from local services and businesses), pictures and posters of people wearing hats for protection, information books about snails, aprons, ready-mixed paint, a wipeable table-top surface, cartridge or sugar paper, coloured mounting paper, tissue paper, pipe-cleaners, PVA glue, scissors, pencils and double-sided tape.

Preparation

Look at the collection of hard hats and helmets. Encourage the children to feel the hats and try them on. Which people wear hard hats to help them with their job? Why do they need to wear hats like this? Discuss who else might wear a hard hat, such as cyclists and horse-riders. Now go outside to find some snails, or look at some pictures. Look at a snail's shell. How does it help to protect the snail? Why does a snail need this protection? Can the children see the pattern on the snail shell? Show them how to make spiral patterns in the air with one finger.

What to do

Ask the children to wear aprons. Put a blob of ready-mixed paint onto the table in front of each child. Show them how to move one finger around to make a spiral pattern in the paint. Lay a piece of paper on top of the paint and smooth it down, then peel it off carefully to see your print. It is usually possible to make another print before adding more paint. Mix colours to create interesting effects, and let the children make at least two prints each. When the prints are dry, cut out a hat shape for each child from two pieces of paper. Staple these together for the children to make snail shell 'hard hats' to wear.

Discussion

How will a hard hat help to keep you safe? Why is it especially important to protect your head? How can you make sure you are safe when riding a bike or perhaps a horse? Are there any other hobbies where a helmet should be worn?

Follow-up activities

✧ Create some more prints using a 'spiral' printing block made from Plastex (Polystyrene sheet). Alternatively, shape some string into spirals and glue it onto a suitable surface to make a printing block.

✧ Draw some large snails' shells on paper and help the children to cut out a section in the middle to open like a door. Stick each shell onto another sheet of paper, leaving the flap open. Let the children draw pictures of what a snail might have in his home inside the flap.

✧ Write a poem about a snail around a large spiral shape.

IN DISGUISE

Objective

PE – To make a mask for using in a dance or parade.

Group size

Up to six.

What you need

Card (for making masks), collage materials including coloured feathers, pasta, Cellophane, sequins, buttons, fabric scraps, pipe-cleaners, corks and ribbons, Marvin medium glue (useful because it dries quickly), bright or fluorescent ready-mixed paints, scissors, lollipop sticks, string, double-sided tape, a hole punch.

all over and leave to dry. The children can glue on a range of collage materials to create the different characters. Use corks for noses and pipe-cleaners for antennae. Make beaks and ears from card leaving a tab for attaching to the mask with double-sided tape. Allow time for the glue to dry. Use a hole punch and string to tie on the masks. For those children who prefer to hold the mask in front of their face, use double-sided tape to fix a lollipop stick at each side of the mask's base.

Play some suitable dance music and hold a mask parade or let the children create a dance based around their character. Encourage them to show what kind of character they are playing by their movements. Will their movements be fast, slow, jerky, smooth, creeping, twisting and turning, prowling, skipping, crawling, jumping, hopping or wriggling? Play a guessing game to find out what type of character each child's mask represents.

Preparation

Prepare for the mask-making activity by cutting some card into oval shapes, large enough to cover a child's face. Then show the children an example of a mask, holding it in front of your face. Does the mask change you in any way? How? Talk about why people wear masks. Have the children seen a carnival or a fancy dress parade? Brainstorm some ideas for mask characters – animals, clowns, monsters, space aliens, insects.

What to do

Ask the children to decide what kind of mask they would like to make. Each child will need help to mark where the eye holes should be in their mask. Mark the spots with a pencil, and let the children draw whatever shape and size of eye they need for their chosen character. Adult help will also be needed to cut out the eye holes. Paint the masks

Discussion

Do masks show your feelings or are they a way of hiding how you feel and who you are? Discuss occasions when the children have worn masks, such as at parties or when playing games. Why did they wear a mask at that time?

Follow-up activities

✧ Try to collect a range of different masks, especially ones from different countries (African masks are generally easy to obtain). Invite the children to bring in any masks they have at home. What materials are they made of? Talk about the different expressions on the masks and see if the children can copy them with their faces.
✧ Look at *Making Faces* by Norman Messenger (Dorling Kindersley).
✧ Sing 'Mask magic' by Sue Nicholls on page 85.

OUR SPECIAL CLOTHES

Objective

RE – To look at special clothes which show that we belong to a group or organisation.

Group size

Whole group.

What you need

Clothes which show membership of an organisation, club or group. Examples could include uniforms for Brownies, Beavers or Boys'/Girls' Brigade members, kits worn at dance or gym classes, football scarves and clothes worn at riding clubs.

Preparation

Ask the children about their hobbies – do they belong to any clubs? Encourage them to bring in their uniform or special clothes to show the whole group. (Send a note to parents first.) Set aside some time, perhaps in an assembly or during circle time, to look at and discuss the clothes.

What to do

Ask the children to model their uniform or special clothes for the rest of the group to look at. Look at any parts of the uniform which are particularly interesting, such as badges. What can the group find out about the organisation the child belongs to by looking at the uniform?

Discussion

Encourage the children to talk about the organisation they belong to. What kind of activities do they do? Do their clothes tell us anything in particular, for example Brownie badges or coloured belts in judo? Can the children describe any clothes they wear to help or protect them in their activity such as leotards for gym, hard hats for riding, shoes for ballet or tap? Do they have friends in their club? Who runs the club and what do they wear? Where do they have to go and how do they get there? Do they have to do anything to keep the uniform or special clothes looking good, such as polish shoes, or dust and shine badges? Talk about being part of a team, helping others in the group and being proud to belong.

Follow-up activities

✧ Draw portraits of the children wearing their uniforms or special clothes. In pairs, write about the organisation or club that the children belong to (ask an adult to scribe for younger children).
✧ Make special badges or hats for the children to wear to show that they belong to your group.
✧ Sing the song 'Uniforms' on page 85.
✧ Learn the poem 'Special clothes for special people' on page 71.

CLOWNS

. . . .

Objective

English – To explore facial expression as part of speaking and listening skills.

Group size

Up to six children.

What you need

Pictures of clowns, the story *Smarty Pants* by Joy Cowley and June Melser (*Story chest* series, Nelson) or any suitable story about clowns, three pieces of stiff card (A1) or three sides of a large box (to make a free-standing 'Aunt Sally' booth), a set of face paints.

Preparation

Make an 'Aunt Sally' booth using three pieces of stiff card fixed together with strong tape. Cut a hole in the front section, large enough for a child to put his or her face through. Paint a picture of a clown around the hole. Enlist the help of a willing parent or other adult to help with painting the children's faces in the activity below.

What to do

Look at the clown pictures and read the *Smarty Pants* story. Smarty Pants the clown is a show-off, and in the story we see how he goes skiing, flying and swimming, taking his poor dog with him! His antics end in trouble as he swings on a vine and hurts his thumb. Show the children Smarty Pants' face in the book. How does he look? How do they think he feels? Does his face tell us how he feels? Ask the children to show a variety of emotions by using their faces. Can they show that they are happy, sad, scared, angry, confused?

Introduce the 'Aunt Sally' game to the children. Show them that when they put their face through the hole, they become a clown. Let them play with the 'Aunt Sally' booth, preferably supervised by an adult. Encourage them to find as many facial expressions as possible.

Ask a parent or other adult to paint the children's faces, using face paints, to create clowns, letting the children choose whether they want a happy or sad face.

Discussion

Encourage the children to talk about their own experiences of clowns and the circus. What kind of clothes do clowns wear? Why do they need special clothes? Do their clothes fit? How do their clothes make clowns look? What sort of colours are clowns' costumes?

Follow-up activities

✧ Learn the song 'When the circus comes to town' *Apusskidu Songs for Children* (A & C Black).
✧ Make bouncy clowns using paper plates for heads, sugar paper folded into a concertina shape for bodies and thin card for boots, hands and hats.
✧ Fold card into cone-shapes and staple together to make clowns' hats for the children to wear. Decorate with tissue-paper bobbles.
✧ Make a happy book and a sad book using children's own drawings and writing.
✧ Make clown faces from clay. Roll and cut out some face shapes (a card template will make this easier). Provide the children with clay tools to stamp and draw on the clown's face. Place small pieces of crumpled newspaper under the faces to raise their centre and support their shape while they dry. Finally, biscuit fire, paint and glaze the clown faces with PVA glue.
✧ Learn the poem 'Who am I?' on page 70.

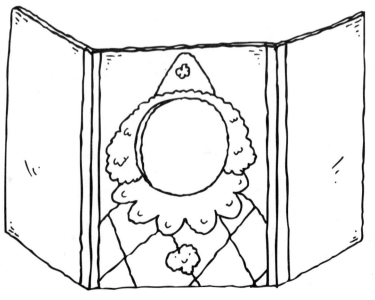

CHAPTER 4
CLOTHES FROM OTHER TIMES AND PLACES

Children can learn that clothes in the past were different to those we wear today. There are also activities to show them the rich variety of clothes worn by people across the globe, from Wales to Japan!

SCOTTISH TARTAN

Objective

Art – To observe and copy tartan patterns.

Group size

Up to eight children.

What you need

Fabrics, clothes and wrapping papers showing a variety of tartan patterns, posters and pictures of Scottish national dress and countryside scenes, cartridge paper (A3), rollers, thin paint brushes, ready-mixed paint, water pots, plastic lids (from large margarine or ice-cream tubs).

Preparation

Set up a display of the different tartan patterns and invite the children to look at them closely. Explain that some different families or 'clans' in Scotland have their own special tartan. (Explain that kilts are usually worn in Scotland on special occasions.) Ask them to look at the different colours in the tartan and how these change where the stripes overlap.

Encourage them to spot squares, rectangles, thin and thick stripes. Set up a table for pattern making. Put out some paint on large plastic lids and provide a roller for each colour. Set out a thin brush, some water and a sheet of paper for each child.

What to do

Demonstrate how to use a roller to spread paint evenly on the plastic lids. Explain that they must keep the roller straight to make a stripe across the paper. Tell them to replace the roller with the handle resting on the table and not in the paint. (Younger children will need an adult's help.) The children can then try using different colours to make criss-cross stripes, watching out for colour changes. When they are happy with their basic pattern, they can paint thin lines in different colours (using a small brush) to accent their stripes. When the tartan patterns are dry, the children can mount them on paper in a contrasting colour. (See page 62 for a full display idea.)

Discussion

Talk about some of the special words associated with tartan and kilts: national dress, pleat, buckle, pin, sporran, tassel, fringe, diamond pattern (particularly on socks). Have the children heard bagpipes being played? Do they know of any special Scottish foods? Have they heard of the Loch Ness monster?

Follow-up activities

✧ Listen to some bagpipe music. Is it happy or sad music? Are the sounds loud or quiet? How do the children think the sounds are made?
✧ Talk about the Loch Ness monster. What kind of place is a loch? Make Plasticine monsters and invent adventures for them.

AIKEN DRUM

Objective

Music – To learn the song 'Aiken Drum' and accompany with percussion.

Group size

Up to fifteen children.

What you need

The song 'Aiken Drum' on page 86, a variety of percussion instruments, ladles and other kitchen equipment such as saucepans, wooden spoons, colanders, chop sticks, tin plates.

Preparation

Teach the song 'Aiken Drum' to the children. Encourage them to make up their own verses in the same format. Look at the instruments or kitchen equipment and teach the children what each item or instrument is called and how to play it.

What to do

Provide fifteen instruments or kitchen items, including three or four ladles, for each child to choose from. Sing the song 'Aiken Drum' and ask only the children with ladles to join in at the line 'he played upon a ladle, a ladle, a ladle' in the first verse. Let the rest of the children join in with their instruments for the other verses. You can change the first verse each time, with Aiken Drum playing on a tambourine, triangle or symbol, for example. Including kitchen equipment such as a saucepan, a wooden spoon, a colander or chopsticks will add to the children's enjoyment! Alter the selection of instruments you offer each time accordingly, and make sure that each child has an opportunity to play an instrument.

Discussion

What do you think would happen to Aiken Drum's clothes if it rained? Would he be able to keep warm in the cold? What would happen to cream cheese if the weather was hot? What food would you like to dress in? What do astronauts wear when they go to the moon?

Follow-up activities

✧ Paint or draw pictures of Aiken Drum wearing his strange clothes in each verse. Let the children sing the song to the rest of the class or group, holding up their pictures to show what Aiken Drum looks like.
✧ Draw a 'man in the moon' on black paper using pastel crayons.
✧ What kind of place do the children think the moon is? Find some pictures of the moon's surface. Talk about astronauts and the clothes they wear when they go to the moon. Why do they need special clothes? How do the astronauts travel to the moon?

COMPARING QUEENS

Objective

History – To compare pictures of Queen Elizabeth I and Queen Elizabeth II.

Group size

Whole group.

What you need

A collection of photographs and pictures of Elizabeth II, including stamps and coins and a formal 'portrait-style' picture, a copy of 'The Phoenix Portrait' of Elizabeth I by Nicholas Hilliard.

Preparation

Talk to the children about the pictures of Elizabeth II. Do they know who she is? (If you have done the activity on page 27, the children will be more familiar with who the Queen is and her role today.) What job do they think the Queen does? What sort of clothes is she wearing in the pictures? Does she always wear a crown? Do they know the names of some other members of the Royal family? Are the pictures paintings or photographs?

What to do

Show the children the portrait of Elizabeth I by Nicholas Hilliard. Explain that she was a queen who lived a long time ago in England. Encourage the children to look at it carefully. Is it a painting or a photograph? Do they think there are any photographs of Elizabeth I? Why not? Compare the clothes worn by Elizabeth I in the portrait and those worn by Elizabeth II in the pictures. How are they different? Which clothes do the children prefer? (Do this activity over several short sessions with younger children to help them keep their concentration.)

Display the portrait of Elizabeth I clearly in front of the children again and play an 'I Spy' type game to develop their observation skills. Focus on details, saying, 'I spy a lace collar,' for example, and ask the children to point it out on the portrait. Continue the game, focusing on the pearl beads on the necklace (count them), the brooch (look at the detail), the veil and so on.

Discussion

Do the children think Queen Elizabeth I was pleased with her portrait? Talk about the Queen's face. Do the children think it looks like a mask? Explain that Elizabeth I wore special white make-up to create this effect. Do the children think that Elizabeth I always looked like this or did the painter make her look nicer in his picture? Does she look rich or poor? How can they tell? Do they like the way she looks or do they prefer the pictures of Queen Elizabeth II?

Follow-up activities

✧ Ask the children to choose a detail from 'The Phoenix Portrait' to copy carefully. Give them magnifying glasses and small card frames so that they can focus on the detail more clearly.
✧ Make collage pictures of Queen Elizabeth I. Decorate the dress with sequins and beads, use gold or silver foil for jewellery and doilies to create a lace effect for the collar. Use strands of orange wool shaped into 'curls' to imitate the hair.
✧ Visit an art gallery to look at some other portraits.
✧ Read 'The Emperor's new clothes' on page 73 and learn the traditional rhyme 'The Queen of Hearts'.

IN THE FUTURE

Objective

Design and Technology – To make some 'futuristic' style clothes from junk/found materials.

Group size

Up to six children.

What you need

A variety of junk materials, including some large (child-sized) cardboard boxes, coloured bin liners (cut a hole in each one large enough to fit over a child's head), rolls of silver/coloured foil, Marvin medium glue (this dries faster than PVA), sticky tape, masking tape, string, a stapler, ready-mixed paint, a large table (for working on), newspaper, a camera and film, an adult to help.

Preparation

Talk to the children about how they think people will dress in the future. Most of them will have seen TV programmes which show futuristic dress and will have some ideas about this. Ask questions like: Will men and women wear different clothes or the same? Will they still wear shoes and hats? What sort of material or fabric will their clothes be made from? What kind of colours will they wear? Will they need special clothes for big occasions? Will they have to wear uniforms? Will their clothes still need to protect them from the weather?

What to do

Ask the children to imagine what sort of clothes the people on planet Earth will wear 200 years from now. Give them plenty of time to suggest ideas, then explain that they are going to make some of these clothes. Provide them with the junk materials to look at. Give them time to decide what they want to make and what materials they will use. Some children will find it difficult to use their imagination and will need a simple idea to start them off. Some ideas may be too ambitious and the child will need adult guidance to translate their ideas into an object that he or she is capable of making. When the children are ready, ask an adult to help them with fixing and joining the materials. If using bin liners as body suits, make sure that holes have been cut out before the child tries to put it on.

The children may need several sessions to finish their clothes. If possible, take photographs of them wearing their finished outfits. Use these to make a book about clothes in the future and add in poems or a story made up by the children.

Discussion

Ask the children to wear their clothes for the rest of the group, describing how they were made and if they have any special purpose.

Follow-up activities

✧ Invent a story together about a child who lives in the future. Describe what her everyday life is like, what kind of house she lives in, the toys and games she plays with, the food she eats and the place where she goes to learn.
✧ Look at pictures of astronauts. What are their clothes like? Is the colour of the fabric light or dark? Do the children think these clothes would be comfortable to wear? Ask the children to draw pictures of astronauts and rockets. Cut out a large moon, cover with silver foil and display the children's pictures around it.

SWIRLING SARIS

Objective

Geography – To look at and try on a sari.

Group size

Up to six children.

What you need

Pictures and books about India, pictures showing Indian costume, a sari, several lengths of colourful fabric (approximately 2 metres), a globe or simple world map.

Preparation

If possible, invite a parent who wears a sari to come in and talk to the children. Explain that saris originally came from a country called India, where they are still worn by many women today. Tell them that India is far away from our country and show them where it is on the globe or map. Ask them how they think you would get to India and what it might be like there. Give them some time to look through pictures and books about India. Include the pictures of saris and ask the children to look especially at the variety of colour and pattern on the different fabrics.

What to do

Show the children that a sari is simply a long piece of fabric. Give them the lengths of fabric, and ask them to try and cover themselves in as many different ways as possible. Give them plenty of time to experiment. Now use a child as a model and explain that you are going to show them how to put on a sari. (It is even better if a parent who wears a sari can demonstrate this.) Ask the child to hold her arms up. Wrap the fabric quite tightly under the arms leaving one long end. Take the long end around to the back and bring it up over the shoulder to the front so that it hangs straight down (see diagram).

Explain that an Indian lady would not use pins for her sari but would wrap it around so well that it would not come undone. Now allow the children to get into pairs to make saris with their fabric.

Discussion

Would the children like to wear saris every day? Did they find it easy to get dressed? What kind of weather is best for wearing a sari?

Follow-up activities

✧ Find some books which show traditional Henna patterns painted on the hands of Indian brides. Let younger children copy them onto paper. Older children should be given the chance to design their own patterns.

✧ Copy some patterns onto the children's hands using face paints.

LONG, LONG AGO

Objective

History – To make a knight's tunic with a coat of arms.

Group size

Up to eight children.

What you need

Books and pictures about knights and heraldry, paper (A4), sheets of sugar paper or thin card (A2) in a variety of colours, paints, pens, pencils, scissors, masking tape.

Preparation

Look at some pictures of knights and coats of arms. Tell the children that a long time ago, men fought battles with each other on horseback. These men were called knights. They wore special clothes called armour to protect them. Armour was made of metal so that the men would not be hurt by spears and axes. The armour was very heavy and difficult to wear. Sometimes the horses wore armour too. Explain that each knight had a special picture or pattern to show which family he came from. He wore a tunic over his armour showing this special pattern which was called his 'coat of arms'. His shield would probably have been painted with this pattern, too. Now prepare a template of the tunic for each child to draw around.

What to do

Explain to the children that they are now going to design their own 'coat of arms' to put on a 'knight's tunic'. Ask younger children to make a random pattern or picture. Encourage older children to think of something important about their own family to include in their picture. Ask them to draw their 'coats of arms', then put the drawings aside until later.

Next, provide the tunic templates for the children to draw round on a large piece of card or paper. Tell them to cut the tunic shape out carefully. (Some children will need help to cut out the head hole.) Fold the tunics at the shoulders. Give the children their original drawings and let them copy a larger version of their pattern onto the front of the tunic. (If this is too difficult, enlarge the original drawings on a photocopier and cut and stick onto the tunic front.) Now the tunics are ready to decorate with paint. When the tunics are dry, let the children try them on. Tape the sides gently with masking tape (this can be peeled off to remove the tunic).

Discussion

Ask the children to imagine that under their tunics they are wearing clothes made of metal (armour). What would this feel like? Would armour bend and move like normal clothes? How do they think a knight moved around or mounted his horse? (Explain that a winch, like a small crane, was often used.) Would armour feel heavy or light, warm or cold? How would a knight have looked after his armour? Do the children think that wearing armour was a good idea? Would it really have protected a knight in battle? Why do they think the knights had battles?

Follow-up activities

✧ Learn the poem 'Five royal knights' on page 72.
✧ Make some shields from stiff card showing the children's 'coat of arms'. Let the children wear their tunics and hold the shields in a special 'coat of arms' parade.
✧ Visit a castle or contact your local museum service to look at some real armour.

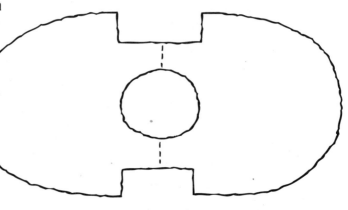

JAPANESE STYLE

Objective

Geography – To look at kimonos and to print patterns onto paper kimono shapes.

Group size

Up to eight children.

What you need

Books and pictures about Japan, clear pictures of Japanese dress, Japanese symbols and writing, a kimono-style dressing gown, paper in various colours (A2), small junk materials (for printing), sponges, ready-mixed paint, printing ink and rollers, large plastic lids (for rolling paint), Plastex (polystyrene sheet for making printing blocks), stiff card, crêpe paper (in different colours), PVA glue, a globe or simple world map.

Preparation

Start by cutting a selection of large kimono shapes from different coloured paper. Next, cut some pieces of Plastex measuring 10cm × 10cm for the older children in the group to use as printing blocks. Then cut some stiff card into pieces measuring 12cm × 12cm. Now prepare a table for printing – for younger children provide a collection of small junk materials, sponges and plates of ready-mixed paint. For older children, set out some rollers and plastic lids or other flat containers for printing ink.

Show the children the pictures and books of Japan. Find Japan and Britain on the globe or world map and mark with a star or arrow. Tell the children that you are going to look at kimonos which are part of the traditional dress in Japan. Show them a kimono if possible. Point out the basic straight line shape of the kimono and explain that it is tied tightly around the middle with a large sash or belt.

What to do

Let each child choose a kimono shape. Younger children can print simple abstract patterns in a variety of colours using the junk materials.

Encourage older children to look closely at some of the Japanese letters and symbols to copy for their printing. Let them draw their symbols or letters onto a piece of Plastex, pressing in well with a pencil but not making a hole right through. Glue the Plastex onto the stiff card to make printing blocks for decorating the kimono shapes. When the ink or paint is dry, ask the children to make a sash from crêpe paper to match their kimonos.

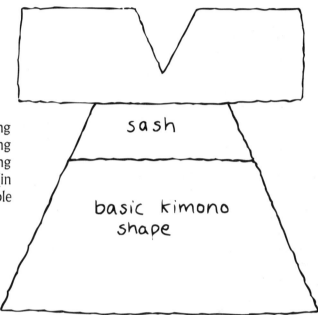

sash

basic kimono shape

Discussion

Do the children think that kimonos can be worn by men as well as by women? Would a kimono be comfortable to wear? What kind of fabric might a kimono be made from? Do they think Japan is a hot or a cold country?

Follow-up activities

✧ Create a display using the kimono shapes. Add some large fans and bamboo parasols. Tell the children about the custom of the Japanese tea ceremony. Set up a small table with plastic cups in front of the display and let the children role-play their own 'tea ceremony' in pairs, perhaps using clothes from the dressing-up box to represent kimonos.

✧ Look at some Japanese prints, especially the famous picture of the sea wave by Hokusai. Do the prints all look very different or are they similar in some way? Older children may like to try doing their own 'Japanese print'.

WELSH HAT GAME

Objective

Geography – To play the 'Welsh hat' game and learn some simple facts about Wales.

Group size

Four children.

What you need

Clear pictures of Welsh traditional costume, books about Wales with pictures of the two Severn crossings and mountains, a map with Wales marked out clearly, a Welsh traditional costume (optional), 4 score cards and 40 hats copied from page 93, a copy of the game on page 94, 4 counters, 1 dice, card, a laminator or some sticky-backed plastic.

Preparation

Photocopy pages 93 and 94 and stick them onto card. Cut out the score cards and hats. Colour in these and the game board and laminate or cover with sticky-backed plastic. Show the children the pictures of Welsh costumes, but make sure they understand that people don't wear national costume all the time, just on special occasions!

What to do

Introduce the Welsh hat game, showing the children that it is based on the map of Wales and that the circles are stepping stones to follow. Put the hats next to the game board and give each child a score card. Let four children at a time play the game with an adult (younger children will need help with reading the game board). They should take it in turns to throw the dice and move round the map on the stepping stones according to their score. They collect hats from the pile as they go, and put these onto their score card. The first child with ten hats is the winner. (Remind the children to keep count of their hats during the game!)

Discussion

As the children progress round the game, the adult can tell them about the different elements which they meet:

• A Welsh cake is a flat scone made on a griddle or 'bakestone'.
• The Severn bridges are made up of the old bridge (a suspension bridge) and a new one (a cable stayed bridge). Have the children crossed the bridge to Wales? What was it like? Did they have to pay? What could they see? Do they know about any other big bridges?
• Look at the Welsh dragon and explain that it is a special emblem for Wales. The children may have seen it on road signs.
• Talk about mountaineering – would the children like to have a go? What is a mountain? Is it different from a hill? What sort of equipment does a mountaineer need?
• Look at the daffodils, also a special emblem for Wales on St David's Day on 1 March.
• Have the children seen sheep wandering freely on hills? How does the farmer know which sheep belong to him?
• Leeks are another special emblem for Wales. Have they ever eaten a leek? How many other vegetables can the children name?
• Cardiff is the most important city in Wales because it is the capital of that country. How many other big cities can the children name?

Follow-up activities

✧ Make some leek and potato soup.
✧ Paint or make a collage of Welsh emblems including daffodils, leeks, red dragons and Welsh hats.
✧ Read *There's No Such Thing as a Dragon* by Jack Kent (Happy Cat Books).

CHAPTER 5
SHOES AND SOCKS

Feet and footprints begin this chapter which goes on to look at types of footwear, fastenings and the colours and sizes that shoes come in.

LOOK AT MY FEET!

Objective

Art – To make footprints using paint.

Group size

Up to ten children.

What you need

The story 'The King with Dirty Feet' by Pomme Clayton from *Time For Telling* (Kingfisher), ready-mixed paint, a large paint tray or meat tin, a long roll of strong paper (for printing on), a bowl of soapy water, a towel, scissors, brightly coloured backing paper, PVA glue, two adults to help.

Preparation

Read 'The King with Dirty Feet' to the children. The story is about a king who has never heard of shoes and so goes around with bare feet. His feet get covered in dust, so he orders his servant to find a way to get rid of the dust. The servant tries this by covering the ground with a leather carpet. An old man shows the king that the carpet will stop plants growing, so instead, he cuts the leather around the king's foot and ties it on with string. The king has the first pair of shoes! Ask the children to take off their shoes and socks and look at their feet. How do they think it would feel to have no shoes? Do they know the names of the different parts of their feet?

What to do

Tell the children that they are going to make some foot prints. Put some ready-mixed paint into a large tray and roll out a long piece of paper. Put the paint tray at one end of the paper and the towel and bowl of warm soapy water at the other end. Encourage a child to stand in the tray with bare feet. Ask an adult to hold on to the child's hands during this activity. Let the child walk carefully along the paper to make footprints. Ask a second adult to wash and dry the child's feet afterwards. Repeat the activity with the other children, using different colours. Once the prints are dry, ask the children to cut them out and use them to make collage pictures on brightly coloured paper.

Discussion

Look at the footprints. What can you tell from seeing them? Do the children have big or little feet? Are their feet narrow or wide? What did the paint feel like to stand in? Was it warm or cold, smooth, sticky, slimy, nice, awful?

Follow-up activities

✧ Make a footprint trail to follow around the room with simple clues to follow.
✧ Mount ten pairs of footprints and use them to help the children count in twos.
✧ Mount one footprint onto the wall and label it clearly with the different parts of the foot.

CINDERELLA'S SHOE SHOP

Objective

Mathematics — To use a role-play shoe shop for work on size and simple sums involving money.

Group size

Whole group, with four children at a time in the 'shoe shop'.

What you need

A traditional version of the Cinderella tale, a role play screen, lots of shoe boxes (try a local shoe shop), card, money, a till, four small purses or containers, each filled with coins totalling 20p, sticky labels for prices, six or more pairs of shoes, slippers and boots in a variety of sizes, felt-tipped pens, crayons or paints, pencils, scissors and glue.

Preparation

Read the story of Cinderella to the children. Talk about why the shoe did not fit the ugly sisters. Ask the children about their shoe size. Where do they go to buy their shoes? Explain that you are now going to make a 'Cinderella's shoe shop' in your room and you need their help with this.

First, brainstorm some ideas, then set up the screen so that the shop area opens out into the room. Collect shoe boxes and shoes ready to fill your shop.

Encourage the children to make advertising posters to decorate the shop walls. Stick price labels (up to 10p) onto the shoe boxes. Arrange the shoes in pairs in the boxes and stand the boots against the shop wall. Make a shoe size chart out of card for measuring customers' feet. You can do this by asking the whole group to take off their left shoe, for example, and look at the size. Draw round one shoe for each size within the group. Label these clearly with the size number. Finally, set up the till with plenty of change and put money into the purses or containers to a total value of 20p. (Provide 1p and 2p coins for younger children and 1p, 2p, 5p, 10p, and 20p coins for older children.)

What to do

Let up to four children at a time use the shop to choose and buy a pair of shoes. Have one child as the shop assistant who measures feet, one child as the cashier to take the money and two children as the customers. (Give a purse to each customer.) Work with the children on coin recognition, addition and change giving. Use the opportunity to bring in lots of basic vocabulary: fit, price, boot, sandal, laces, heel, slipper, sole, leather, canvas, rubber, plastic, tight, loose, comfortable, wide, long.

Discussion

Who takes you to buy shoes? What different types of shoes are available? Why do we need different types of shoes? What kind of shoes do you wear in the summer/winter?

Follow-up activities

✧ Make a large collage picture of Cinderella.
✧ Ask the children to make up a story about a magic pair of shoes that they find. What happens when they put on the shoes?
✧ Organise a visit to a real shoe shop.
✧ Find pictures of shoes that people wore in the past and compare them with the shoes we wear today. (Contact the Clark's Museum in Street, Somerset — see page 96 for details.)
✧ Sing 'The shoe shop' on page 87.

AN ODD SOCK

Objective

English – To make up a story about an odd sock.

Group size

Up to eight children.

What you need

A small washing basket filled with pegs and various pieces of clothing including several pairs of socks, a large, brightly coloured 'odd sock', buttons or 'eyes' (to sew on the sock), card, paper, felt-tipped pens, pencils, crayons, a stapler, scissors.

Preparation

Make a sock-shaped book for each child to write and draw in. Sew the 'eyes' on to the brightly coloured 'odd sock' and place it in the washing basket, mixing it up with the clothes, other socks and pegs. Show the children the washing basket and ask them to help you sort out your washing. Go through the washing, shaking and folding it and putting the socks into pairs. When you come to the odd sock, look surprised, put your hand into it and hold it up to show the children. Say: 'Where

did this sock come from? It doesn't belong to me. I wonder how it got into my washing basket?'

Encourage the children's ideas about the sock. What sort of person might it belong to? How did it get into the washing basket? Where is the sock that goes with it? How will the person manage with only one sock? Where does the person live? Continue to brainstorm until the children collect plenty of ideas.

What to do

Give each child a 'sock book' and tell them that they are going to make up their own story book about the odd sock. The writing will depend on the age of your group. Younger children will need an adult to scribe their story but can add in their own drawings. Help the children to name their characters and to sequence their stories by asking 'What happens next?'.

When the stories are complete, ask the children to colour and decorate the covers using felt-tipped pens in bright colours. Share the finished stories with the rest of the group in class or during assembly time.

Discussion

Why do we wear socks? Do the children have a favourite pair of socks? Do these socks have pictures on? What colour are they? Is it important to wear matching socks or could you wear a different sock on each foot?

Follow-up activities

✧ Record the children's stories on tape and provide these in the 'listening corner' so that other children have access to them.
✧ Fill a washing basket with ten pairs of socks and ask the children to sort them into matching pairs. Use this activity to give them practice in counting in twos.
✧ Learn 'Lost sock' on page 70.

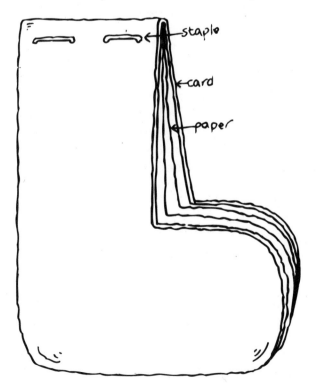

staple

card

paper

HOW DO MY SHOES FASTEN?

Objective

Mathematics — To make charts showing the children's different shoe fastenings.

Group size

Whole group.

What you need

Paper (A2 and A4), felt-tipped pens, scissors, glue sticks.

Preparation

Make a chart by dividing a large sheet of A2 paper into three columns with 15 or more horizontal rows, depending on the number of children in

ask them to write their name on the shoe which fastens in the same way as their own. When they have finished, count up the number of names on each shoe and write the total in a large box on the heel. Mount the shoe shapes onto the wall.

Now show the children the second chart and provide them with the small paper shoe shapes. Ask them to colour these in to match the shoes they are wearing. Explain that you want them to stick their shoe shape on to the correct column in the chart to show what type of fastening their shoe has. When they have finished, label the top of each column to show the totals. Display the charts clearly for the children to see.

Discussion

Ask the children to look carefully at the charts. Can they tell which shoe fastening is the most popular? Which fastening is used the least often? How many shoes are on the chart altogether? Which chart do they find easiest to understand?

your group. Write three clear labels: 'buckles', 'lace-ups' and 'Velcro'. Stick one label at the bottom of each of the three columns. Cut enough small shoe shapes for each child to fit into a space on the chart. Then, draw three large shoe shapes on paper and cut them out. Prepare the same three labels as for the chart above and stick one onto each shoe shape.

What to do

Tell the children that you are going to make a chart of how everyone's shoes fasten. Ask them to take off one shoe and look at how it fastens. Is it tied with laces, fixed with Velcro or hooked into a buckle? Show them the three large shoe shapes and

Can they think of any other ways to do shoes up? Do all shoes need to be done up? Talk about the colours of the shoes on the large chart. How many children have black shoes? How many have brown? What is the most popular colour?

Follow-up activities

✧ How many children can do up laces? Make a chart and provide some old lace-up shoes for them to have a go with.
✧ Shoes and socks are always in pairs. What other things come in pairs? Make a collection of these items.
✧ Read the story 'Sunday boots and working boots' on page 75.

WHAT A LOT OF SHOES!

Objective

Music – To make percussion sounds.

Group size

Up to six children.

What you need

A good selection of percussion instruments, a tape recorder and tape, the poem 'What a lot of shoes'.

Preparation

Provide the selection of percussion instruments for the children to look at. What sound does each one make? Is there a special way to hold each instrument? Do they know what each instrument is called? Provide some time for the children to experiment with the instruments and to become familiar with the sounds each one can make. Now teach them the poem 'What a lot of shoes', emphasising the sound words, perhaps using actions or body percussion:

> ### What a lot of shoes
>
> My mum's high heels go tip tip tip
> My dad's big boots go clump clump clump
> My sister's sandals go flip flop flip
> My brother's trainers go jump jump jump
> But my little feet go pitter, pitter pat
> Can you make a sound like that?
> *Anne Piper*

What to do

Decide with the children which instrument to use for each sound in the poem. For example 'tip tip tip' could be a lightly tapped triangle, 'clump clump clump' could be a tambourine. Let each child choose from the relevant selection of instruments and go through the poem asking them to add the appropriate percussion sounds. The children can take it in turns to be the conductor, signalling the beginning and end of the poem.

Discussion

Tape a performance of the percussion poem. Talk about each instrument and why it was chosen to make that sound. Perhaps the children can make up new lines to add, for example, 'Football boots go kick, kick, kick', 'Wellie boots go splish, splash, splosh' and so on.

Follow-up activities

✧ Set up a 'sounds table' with percussion instruments for the children to practise making different sounds. Ask them to choose instruments to create different atmospheres such as a stormy sea, a sunny day, or a birthday party.
✧ Play a listening game. Put some simple everyday objects inside a cardboard box. Can the children guess what is making the sound?
✧ Make some cards showing the names of percussion instruments. Ask the children to match these labels to the correct instrument.
✧ Learn the poems 'Let's do the flip-flop frolic!' on page 67 and 'Shoes' on page 69.

SOCK PUPPETS

Objective

Drama — To make a sock puppet to encourage speaking and listening skills.

Group size

Up to eight children.

What you need

A collection of old clean socks, buttons and small circles of coloured fabric (to make 'eyes'), wool, felt, large sewing needles or crewels (for older children only), cotton thread, scissors, PVA glue.

Preparation

Show the children the collection of socks. Encourage them to talk about the colours, patterns and sizes. Place one sock on your hand in glove puppet fashion and move it around. Say to the children: 'This sock almost seems to be alive! I wonder if we could give it a face. What could we use for eyes, a nose, a mouth and hair? Encourage the children's suggestions. Show them the collection of materials. Can they think of any other materials that would be useful? Add in any other suitable items that they suggest, then explain that they are going to have the chance to make their own sock puppet. Ask each child to choose a sock and let them play

with it on one hand, allowing them plenty of time to develop 'a character'.

What to do

Provide the final selection of materials for the children to choose from. Help them to sew or stick different features onto their socks to make a puppet. Ensure that there is close adult supervision whenever the children are working with needles, and gather them back in as soon as they have finished sewing.

Once the puppets are ready, let the children spend time playing with them, making up conversations and so on. Allow them to play freely, rather than trying to impose a game or a drama on them.

Discussion

Let the children show their puppets to the rest of the group. Ask them what their puppet is called. Now direct some questions to the puppet rather than the child: Where do you live? What do you eat? Are you happy or sad? Do you have any friends?

Follow-up activities

✧ Look at some real examples of different puppets, including string puppets, hand puppets, shadow puppets and rod puppets. Alternatively, find out about them using books and posters.
✧ Try to arrange a visit to a puppet show, or alternatively, put on your own performances using the children's sock puppets.
✧ Ask if the children know the story of Pinnochio the puppet. Can they tell you what happens to him? Read them the story or show them an animated version on video.
✧ Read the story of 'The red sock' on page 77.
✧ Learn the poem 'Socks' on page 70.

MATCHING SOCKS

Objective

Mathematics – To practise matching patterns and making pairs.

Group size

Up to twelve children.

What you need

Eight or more pairs of socks, copies of photocopiable page 95, crayons, pencils, scissors, a laminator or some sticky-backed plastic.

Preparation

Mix up the collection of socks. Ask the children to find the pairs, matching by colour, pattern and size. Once they have had some practice in matching pairs, hand each of them a copy of photocopiable page 95.

What to do

Ask the children to look carefully at the worksheet. Explain that you want them to match the socks into pairs by looking at the patterns. Show them how to link the socks together using a pencil line. They should then colour the socks carefully to match. To finish, they need to identify the child wearing those socks at the top or bottom of the sheet, again linking them with a pencil line. (Younger children will need adult help to complete their sheet.) Extend the activity for older children by cutting out the socks, laminating them and using them for a snap game.

Discussion

Talk about pairs. How many other pairs can the children think of? Suggestions could include eyes, ears, gloves, shoes, trousers and spectacles. Look at everybody's socks. Are all the children wearing a matching pair? Does it matter if each sock has a different pattern or colour? What about if they are different sizes? How do you think this would feel? Do the children's feet match? Are they both exactly the same size?

Follow-up activities

✧ Arrange socks in number groups from one to ten. Make some number labels with words and numbers from one to ten. Spread them on the

table and ask the children to match the correct label to each group of socks.
✧ Display a number line on the wall to help the children count in twos.

THE ELVES AND THE SHOEMAKER
....

Objective

Design and Technology – To make a shoe or sandal.

Group size

Up to six children.

What you need

The story of 'The elves and the shoemaker' on page 78, thick card or construction paper, tape measure, Marvin medium glue, double-sided tape, masking tape, a hole punch, scissors, cutters for thick card, pencils, felt-tipped pens, paints, collage materials including sequins, laces, ribbons, bows, buttons (for decoration), an adult helper.

Preparation

Read 'The elves and the shoemaker' to the children. This is a tale about a poor shoemaker who is helped by two elves. The elves make shoes for him to sell, he then becomes rich and lives happily ever after. The story describes how the shoemaker cuts leather into shapes ready to make shoes. Show the children a real shoe and point out how many parts are sewn and glued together.

Ask the children to look at their own shoes. Where is the heel? Where is the toe? Where does the shoe fasten up?

What to do

Tell the children that they are going to make a shoe or sandal from card and paper and decorate it in their own way. Help each child to place one shoe on some thick card and draw round it to make a template. Draw a second outline for them about 1.5cm outside the first, then cut out the template using the card cutters. (An adult will need to do this for younger children.) Now each child has a base on which to make their shoe or sandal.

Use the construction paper to make the straps and other shapes for the uppers (see diagram), being careful to measure the child's foot each time. (It may be helpful to provide younger children with pre-cut strips, squares, triangles and so on.) Fix the uppers using double-sided tape and masking tape or Marvin glue. The children can now decorate their shoes using pens, paint and collage materials.

Discussion

Ask the children to describe how they made their shoes. Do they look good? Do they fit? Was it difficult to make the shoe? Would they like to be a shoemaker? Which shoes do they enjoy wearing? Are some shoes more comfortable than others?

Follow-up activities

✧ Make a display using a story book of *The Elves and the Shoemaker* and the shoes made by the children, with drawings, paintings and writing to follow up. (See page 61 for details on how to create a full display based around the shoemaker story.)

✧ Contact Clark's Shoe Museum in Street, Somerset (see page 96) for information about the history of shoes. Contact your local museum to arrange a visit to see shoes from other historical times.

CHAPTER 6
HOW CLOTHES ARE MADE

The aim of this chapter is to look at the construction and colour of clothes through activities based around simple pattern making, weaving and fabric dying.

HOW DOES IT FEEL?

Objective

English – To make and use a 'feely box' game and use descriptive vocabulary.

Group size

Up to ten children.

What you need

A cardboard box with a lid (a photocopier paper box is just right), strong wrapping paper in bright colours, a blindfold (optional), examples of fabrics with different tactile qualities such as velvet, sacking, silk, knitted fabric, plastic, leather, fine netting, binca, crinkly cheesecloth, fur fabric, sequinned fabric, scissors, glue, sticky tape.

Preparation

Make the 'feely box' by fixing the lid on the cardboard box and cutting a hole large enough for a child's hand in one end. (You could draw a face on this end with the hole as the mouth.) Cover the box with wrapping paper to make it look interesting. Cut each fabric sample into a square measuring approximately 15cm.

What you do

This activity is especially helpful for children who find using descriptive words difficult. Show the children the 'feely box' and the blindfold. Tell them that you are going to put something into the box. Someone is then going to wear the blindfold or close their eyes tightly and put a hand into the box to feel what is inside. Explain clearly that you want them to describe how the object feels rather than

tell you what it is. Now choose a child to wear the blindfold. Put the fabric sample in the box and ask him or her to feel what is inside the box. You will need to do this activity several times for some children to understand exactly what you want them to do.

Discussion

This activity can be used to bring in some rich descriptive vocabulary: soft, smooth, silky, rough, tickly, slippery, warm, cold, fluffy, ridged, crinkly, woolly, holey, slimy, bendy, stiff. Let the children also invent their own words to describe the fabric if they wish.

Follow up activities

✧ Make a book of all the 'describing words' that the children have used or talked about in the 'feely box' activity. Can the children apply some of these words to other objects?
✧ Make a tactile collage using pieces of the 'feely box' fabric. Put labels around it describing how each fabric feels, or invent simple poems using descriptive words.
✧ Play another blindfold game such as 'Pin the tail on the donkey'.

A FUNNY HAT

Objective

English – To make a 'memory hat'.

Group size

Up to eight children.

What you need

The poem 'Old John Muddlecombe' on page 69, thin card or sugar paper (A2), magazines and catalogues (containing simple everyday objects), scissors, sticky tape, glue.

Preparation

Teach the poem 'Old John Muddlecombe' to the children, complete with the actions. Talk about remembering things. Old John Muddlecombe forgot where he put his hat – have the children ever forgotten where something is? Who helps them to remember? What other ways can help us to remember things? For example, does your mum or dad write lists of shopping or jobs to do?

What to do

Tell the children that they are going to make a special hat to use for a memory game. Let each child choose a piece of paper to make their hat. Bend this round for them into a cone shape to fit on their head and stick with tape. Let each child choose six pictures of different objects from a catalogue or magazine to cut out and stick onto their hat. (Make sure that they don't simply cut out six pictures of the same object that they like!)

When the hats are made, ask the children to choose a partner to play the memory game. Explain how to play the game as follows: 'Put your own hat on your head and ask your partner to look carefully at the pictures on it. Now put your hat on your partner's head. Can your partner remember all the pictures on your hat?' Let each pair repeat the activity again using the other child's hat. Increase or decrease the number of pictures according to the abilities and age of the children.

Discussion

Talk to the children about the game. How many things did they remember? Was it easy or did they forget some of the pictures? Can they remember what they had for breakfast? Can they remember what they did yesterday or at the weekend? Can they remember what is in their bedroom or another room at home?

Follow up activities

✧ Play 'Kim's game' by placing a variety of objects on a tray. Give the children time to try and memorise the objects, then cover the tray with a cloth. How many objects can the children remember?

✧ With older children play the game 'I went to market'. Sit in a circle and start them off by saying, 'I went to the market and bought an apple,' for example. The child next to you has to think of an item, a banana for example, and say, 'I went to the market and bought an apple and a banana'. Continue going round the circle.

✧ Learn a short poem or song together. Who can remember it and say it on their own?

HOW WAS IT MADE?

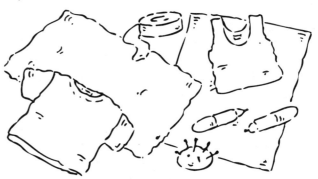

Objective

Design and Technology – To make a simple paper pattern based on a real vest or T-shirt and use it to make another garment.

Group size

Up to ten children.

What you need

A few simple garments such as a T-shirt, skirt and waistcoat, a small child's old vest or T-shirt with side seams (to take apart), fabric (to make a new vest) scissors, a sheet of paper (A2), felt-tipped pens, pins or sticky tape, an adult helper.

Preparation

Show the garments to the children. How do they think the clothes were made? Look for seams and stitches inside the clothes. Follow the seams to see how many pieces of fabric were needed to make each garment. Explain to the children that clothes are made using a pattern or template. In this way, each piece of fabric can be cut out in the correct shape and size. The different pieces are then sewn together to make the finished garment.

What to do

Show the children the old vest or T-shirt. Tell them that you are going to take the garment apart and use it to make a paper pattern. Turn it inside out and ask a child to find the seams and follow them with one finger. Next, cut along the seams carefully with sharp scissors. Separate the pieces and look at the shapes and sizes. Spread the pieces out on a large piece of paper and pin or tape them to keep them steady. Use a felt-tipped pen to draw carefully round the edges of each section. Remove the pieces of garment and cut out the paper pattern. Ask the children how they think this pattern could be used to make a new vest. Once they have suggested some ideas, use the pattern to cut out a new fabric vest or T-shirt and sew together.

Discussion

Talk to the children about patterns for clothes. Why do they think patterns are needed? What would happen if you just guessed at the shape or size when making a garment? Look at the paper pattern made during the activity. Is it exactly the same size as the original garment? Bring in some simple vocabulary: front, back, top, bottom, armhole, neck, stitches, seams, fabric.

Follow-up activities

✧ Staple the paper pattern together to make a paper vest for a large teddy bear.
✧ Learn the poem 'Second best' on page 72.

WEAVING

• •

Objective

Design and Technology – To weave with paper.

Group size

Up to eight children.

What you need

Fabric samples clearly showing the weave (such as sacking), construction paper in a variety of bright colours (A3), glue sticks, scissors, a ruler, a pencil, bright card (for making frames), pieces of narrow ribbon.

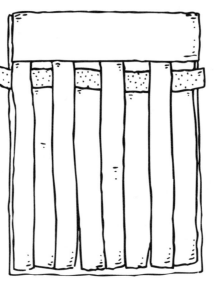

Preparation

Position the A3 paper so that it is landscape. Rule a 3cm margin on the left side. Rule a series of horizontal lines, each 2cm apart, from the opposite side up to the margin. Prepare several pieces in this way to give children a choice of colours. Next, cut lots of 2cm wide strips across the width of A3 paper in different colours (for weaving).

Show the children some examples of fabric where the weave can be clearly seen, such as a piece of sacking, loosely-woven cotton and so on. Point out how the threads weave in and out, some going up and down and some going from side to side. Show the children how they can 'weave' using their fingers and a piece of ribbon. Stick the fingers of one hand up straight and weave the ribbon in and out of the fingers. This will help to introduce the idea of the weaving process.

What to do

Explain that the children are going to use paper strips to weave and make patterns with. Let each child choose a piece of the ready-ruled paper and cut the strips up as far as the margin. Using a glue stick, help them to stick the margin down onto another sheet of uncut A3 paper to keep it steady. Provide them with the ready-cut coloured strips of paper. Now the children can begin to weave the coloured strips in and out across their sheet of paper, pushing the strips up tight against each other. (Some children will find the eye and hand co-ordination needed for this activity difficult, so give them plenty of adult help.) Older children can weave repeat patterns.

Discussion

How did the children weave their paper? What colours did they choose? Introduce the vocabulary 'warp' and 'weft', explaining that warp goes from top to bottom and weft weaves in and out.

Follow-up activities

✧ Use bright card to make frames in interesting shapes such as a fish, an apple and a leaf. Stick these over the children's completed paper weaving and cut to shape.
✧ Find some pictures of fabric being hand-woven on a loom. Ask the children if they think that all fabric is made like this today. Why might it not be possible to weave all fabrics by hand?
✧ Weave with a selection of found materials using a large weaving frame.

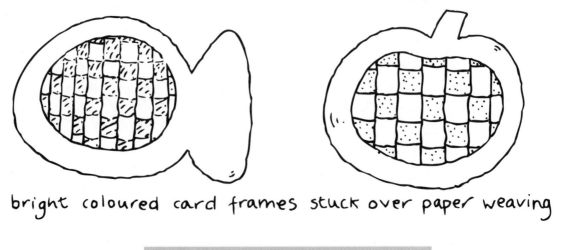

bright coloured card frames stuck over paper weaving

DO YOU LIKE MY BROOCH?

Objective

Design and Technology – To make a simple brooch to wear.

Group size

Up to four children.

What you need

A collection of brooches and badges, some plastic embroidery canvas, large sewing needles, lots of brightly coloured wool or thread, sequins, buttons, PVA glue, safety pins, an adult helper.

Preparation

Cut the plastic canvas into simple shapes such as squares, triangles and circles measuring approximately 5cm × 5cm. Make a collection of brooches and badges for the children to look at.

What to do

Show the children your collection of badges and brooches. Ask them why we like to wear these items. Talk about the different reasons, including how we like to look nice, show that we belong to a group, tell people our name or age, or even tell a joke. Now say that the children are going to make their own special brooch. Show them the canvas shapes and ask them to choose one. Thread a needle and demonstrate how they must push it through the holes and pull the thread all the way through. Encourage them to cover the canvas shapes with random stitches in lots of different colours. (Plenty of adult help will be needed with this, especially to tie off the threads.) When the stitches are complete, the children can decorate the brooch by sticking on sequins or sewing on buttons.

Attach a safety pin to the back of the badge with small stitches (this should be done by an adult). The brooch is then ready to wear.

Discussion

Let the children show their brooches to show the rest of the group. Encourage them to explain how their brooch was made, what colours they chose, what shape their brooch is and so on.

Follow-up activities

✧ Ask the children to bring in a badge or brooch from home to add to your collection. Look at the materials the badges / brooches are made from. What material is used the most often? Which material is used the least often?

✧ Ask older children if they have a special badge, for example one they bought from a favourite place they visited, or a badge given to them by someone special. Ask them to wear it for the other children and to explain why this is their favourite badge.

CLOTHES LABELS

Objective

Mathematics – To design some symbols for clothes labels.

Group size

Up to six children.

What you need

A variety of children's clothes, paper (A3), black handwriting pens.

Preparation

Set out the collection of children's clothes and let the group look at the labels inside. What do they tell you? Look for shop names, sizes, fabric names and washing instructions. Draw some of the symbols on a white board or large piece of paper. Can the children tell you what they mean? Now explain that you want them to invent some symbols of their own to show what size a garment is and how to wash it.

What to do

Give each child some instructions on what sort of clothes label to design, for example 'show it's for a big person', 'show it's for a little person', 'show that it can be washed in a machine'. When the children have designed their symbols, sit in a circle

and spread out the labels so everyone can see them. Ask each child to explain what their own symbols mean. Next, put together one of the size labels and two of the washing instructions designed by the children. Can anyone tell you what the symbols mean?

Discussion

Why do we need labels in our clothes? What do they tell us? Do the children think labels are important? What would happen if there were no labels in our clothes?

Follow-up activities

✧ Mount the children's symbols in groups and display next to articles of clothing or paintings of different clothes.

✧ Collect some stories about big, middle-sized and small things, for example 'Goldilocks and the Three Bears' and 'The Three Billy Goats Gruff'.

✧ Read *Doing the Washing* by Sarah Garland (Puffin).

WHAT COLOUR IS IT?

Objective

Art – To tie-dye a piece of fabric with two colours.

Group size

Up to six children.

What you need

A few items of clothing in plain bright colours, white 100% cotton sheeting, two Dylon cold dyes in bright colours, salt, a large clothes line, pegs or a painting dryer, two large buckets, a pair of rubber gloves, newspaper, aprons, scissors, string, elastic bands.

Preparation

Mix up two buckets of cold dye according to the maker's instructions and add salt for a fixative. Cut the cotton sheeting into A4-sized squares (one for each child). Keep the buckets of dye in the sink area or on a surface which is a well protected with newspaper. Cut lots of lengths of string, each measuring approximately 50cm. Prepare a piece of fabric ready to tie-dye to show the children how it is done. Pinch the fabric together at its centre point and scrunch it up. Wind some string around the fabric at this point and tie tightly. Continue to tie at regular intervals along the length of the fabric, scrunching it together as you go.

Show the children the brightly coloured articles of clothing. How do they think the clothes became that colour, did someone paint the colour on? Explain that clothes are coloured with special colours called dye. The dye does not wash away from the clothes when you put them in the washing machine. Explain that the children are now going to have the chance to dye some material in a way that will make patterns on it.

What to do

The children must wear aprons for this activity! Show them the piece of fabric which you have prepared. Explain that you have tied it really tightly so that the dye can't get to the fabric under the string. Then give each child a piece of the fabric.

Ask them to find the centre and pinch it up, scrunching the fabric together. Now tell them to wind the string round as tightly as possible and tie the ends (adult help will be needed). Use several pieces of string on each piece of fabric. (Children with co-ordination problems could use elastic bands tightened by an adult.) When the children have tied their fabric, write their names in biro on card and staple them to the ends of the strings. Immerse the fabric in the dye bucket and leave until the next day. When the fabric has been dyed, let the children undo their piece, rinse it in cold water and hang it up to dry.

Repeat the process with the second colour. (Using two colours gives interesting colour mixing effects and can lead to other work on colour mixing.)

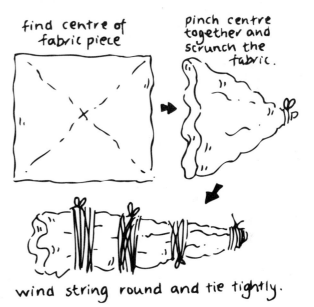

find centre of fabric piece

pinch centre together and scrunch the fabric.

wind string round and tie tightly.

Discussion

Ask the children to show the rest of the group their tie-dyed fabric and explain how it was done. Which colour did they use first? If they could have some tie-dyed clothes, what would they choose to wear and what colour would the clothes be?

Follow-up activities

✧ Make a display of tie-dyed clothes. These are always popular and you can encourage the children to bring in examples.
✧ Sew all the tie-dyed squares together like a patchwork quilt. Cut out each child's initial from felt and stick it onto their own square. Use it as a wall hanging or curtain.

BAA, BAA, BLACK SHEEP

Objectives

Geography – To learn about sheep and their environment. To make a book about wool.

Group size

Up to six children.

What you need

A collection of woollen clothes, balls of coloured wool, raw sheep wool/fleece, pictures and books about sheep and wool, thin card and paper (A4), black sugar paper, cotton wool, glue, felt-tipped pens, pencils, crayons, scissors, clothing catalogues or magazines, the rhyme 'Baa, baa, black sheep'.

Preparation

Make one sheep-shaped book for each child to use. Fold some A4 card and paper in half. With the fold at the top, outline the shape of a sheep and cut out. Staple the paper and card together along the fold. (The size of the books and number of pages will depend on the age of the children. Older children will need more pages. Younger children may need the books to be larger.)

Sing 'Baa, baa, black sheep' with the children and go through the rhyme to find out what it means. Look at the books and pictures about sheep. How much do the children already know? Do they know the words 'ram', 'ewe' and 'lamb'? Where do they think sheep live? What do they eat? What sound do they make? Who looks after them? What does a sheep-dog do?

Next, look at the sheep wool and encourage the children to handle it and feel its natural oiliness. Do they know what a sheep's wool can be made into? How do they think a sheep's fleece becomes the wool that we use to knit with?

What to do

Give each child a sheep-shaped book. Provide the cotton wool and black sugar paper and ask the children to stick these materials onto their book cover to make it look more like a real sheep. They can add in legs made from the sugar paper and draw on a face with a felt-tipped pen. Now encourage them to draw pictures of clothing made from wool on each page or cut out pictures from magazines and catalogues.

This activity can be kept very simple for the younger children, while older children will be able to write and draw in their books to record what they have found out.

Discussion

Encourage the children to explain what their own 'sheep' books are about, then move on to more general questions: Do they like the feel of woolly clothes? Do woollen clothes feel soft or itchy? Is wool warm or cool to wear? Would they wear wool in the summer?

Follow-up activities

✧ Arrange a visit to a sheep farm or animal centre at lambing time.
✧ Read *Emma's Lamb* by Kim Lewis (Walker Books).
✧ Contact your nearest crafts centre and see if they know of a local craftsperson who uses a spinning wheel. You could also invite a parent or grandparent in to do some knitting.
✧ Sing 'A big ball of wool' on page 87.
✧ Learn the poem 'My jumper' on page 72.

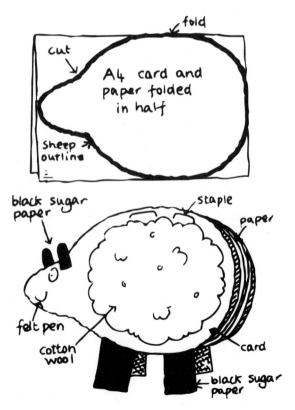

CHAPTER 7
DISPLAYS

Displays can extend the children's learning, reinforce their feelings of 'ownership' and self-esteem, and are informative for parents and visitors. This chapter gives general ideas on presentation, as well as ideas for three specific displays.

Whenever you are setting up a display think carefully about its overall purpose. You may want to use your display as a starting point to an activity to generate interest and provide a stimulus for the children. Alternatively, you may want to use your display to pull together all the children's work at the end of your topic. Either way, your display is bound to provide an attractive focal point which will create a certain atmosphere and encourage discussion. Displaying the children's work also gives them the message that you value what they have created.

Your displays will be for the children themselves, their parents and other visitors to the your group. They are a way of showing parents and visitors what is happening in your group on a day to day basis, and give the children a chance to explain their work to their friends and family. If you intend the children to use the display and interact with it, make sure it is accessible to them and at the appropriate height. This kind of display may not look perfect all the time as it is a working display.

Involve the children in making a display as much as possible. They are all able to play an active part by choosing backing paper, arranging materials and collecting suitable items. Plan displays in advance so that there is plenty of time to gather ideas and collect all the materials needed. It is important to mount the children's work carefully, making the most of colour, shape and texture. Small details such as using a staple gun rather than drawing pins, and adding a border around the display board will make all the difference to the final effect you create.

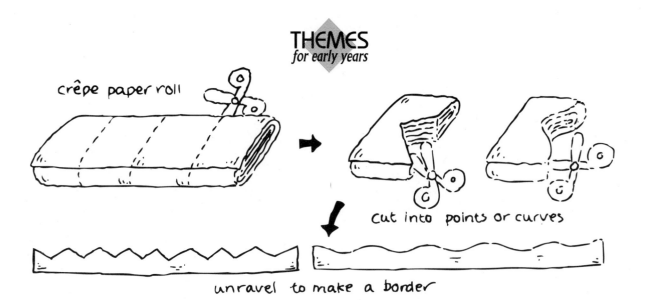

crêpe paper roll

cut into points or curves

unravel to make a border

A good display will invite questions and comments and present the familiar in an unusual way. Remember though that once a display has 'become part of the wallpaper', it is time to make a change.

Setting up

You may find it useful to keep a set of tools in a tool box. Include a good stapler, staple gun, double-sided tape, Blu-tack, string, scissors with long blades, thin and thick lettering pens, craft knife, pins, long-necked drawing pins, Velcro, a light hammer, cup hooks and a bradawl. It is also useful to have available a few plate stands and some word stands to display labels.

Corrugated paper or card will stand up on its own and provide a good background for a display. Fabric, or pieces of sheeting are useful especially if your surface is old and damaged.

Always aim for variety with your displays, positioning items at different levels to take the eye to the focal point. Try using boxes with lengths of fabric draped over them to make levels.

Helpful hints

• When using a staple gun, don't press it down flat against the wall. Hold it out at a slight angle as this makes the staples easier to remove.
• Crêpe paper makes excellent borders for display boards. Cut across the whole roll to make four equal pieces. Cut curves, squares or points into each piece and unravel.
• Create 3D effects by stuffing wads of scrunched-up newspaper behind figures or animals, or mount the children's work onto cereal boxes and staple firmly onto the wall. Stiff cardboard folded into a concertina can also make an interesting 3D mount.

• Make all lettering clear. Invest in a set of large wooden stencils in capitals and lower case. If drawing letters by hand, use pencil guidelines to keep the letter size consistent. Use interesting paper to cut your letters from – sparkly wrapping paper is effective. Choose colours which contrast strongly with your background for maximum impact. Foil letters ready punched are expensive to buy, but if laminated can be used many times. Frame or mount lettering for extra impact.
• If necessary, fix up the display pictures temporarily with pins to work out spacing before you staple.
• A large picture of a famous work of art or a colourful poster makes a good focal point for a display.
• Simple, uncluttered displays are often the most effective.

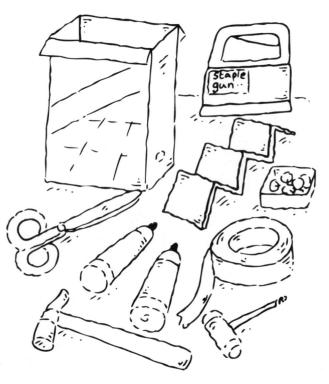

THE ELVES AND THE SHOEMAKER

What you need

A smart pair of shoes, 'The elves and the shoemaker' story, the children's junk material shoes (from the activity on page 50), an old pair of shoes (to make a shoe print border), paper (A3), pencils, paints, a display board and table, bright coloured backing paper, fabric (to cover the table), letter stencils, wrapping paper with pictures of shoes or boots (optional), three shoe boxes with lids, ready mixed-paint and paint tray, a large piece of fabric (to drape one side of the display board).

Preparation

Cover your display board with bright backing paper and the table with a plain cloth which tones in with the display board. Cover the painting table with newspaper and place the old shoes and tray of ready-mixed paint on it. Provide several large pieces of paper for each child to make shoeprints. Staple the fabric across the top right-hand corner of the board and drape it back like a curtain. Cut out the title 'The Elves and the Shoemaker' using letter stencils and wrapping paper.

What to do

Stick some bright new labels onto the shoe boxes. Put the smart shoes into one shoe box and display in the centre of the table with the lid underneath and a label saying 'Today's special shoes, handmade by elves, £100'. Place some of the junk material shoes made by the children on or in the other boxes and label them, for example 'Sandals, made by James, £50', and so on. Paint large pictures of the shoemaker, his wife and the elves in the story. Cut them out when they are dry. Give the children the old shoes and tray of ready-mixed paint. Let them take it in turns to dip the shoe soles in paint to make shoeprints. When the prints are dry, ask the children to cut them out to make a border for the display. Staple all the figures onto the display board with the shoemaker and his wife peeping out from behind a curtain. Encourage the children to write about the story, mount their work and add to the display. Place the story book on the table.

Discussion

How did the elves know how to make shoes? Did they like the clothes that were made for them? How do you think the shoemaker felt when he found the first lovely pair of shoes? What would you have done to help the elves?

SCOTLAND

• •

What you need

Black and fluorescent yellow backing paper, tartan wrapping paper (to use as a border) some tartan clothes (optional), a picture of someone in Scottish national costume, the children's tartan patterns (from the activity on page 35), a display board and table, a tartan rug or table cloth, white sticky labels, a staple gun, glue sticks, scissors.

Preparation

Cover the display board with fluorescent yellow backing paper and make a border using the tartan wrapping paper. Stand the table in front of the display board and cover with the tartan rug or cloth. Make another level using a box on the right-hand side of the table. Display the poster of traditional Scottish costume in the bottom left-hand corner of the display board. Label clearly, for example 'A Scottish person wearing Scottish national costume'. Use large letter stencils to write 'tartan' on the wrapping paper and cut out the individual letters. Staple or glue the letters across the top of the display board.

What to do

Ask the children to mount their tartan patterns (see page 35) on black backing paper. Show them how to cut these out leaving a narrow frame around the edge. Younger children will need help with this.

Let each child write their name on a sticky label and stick it onto a bottom corner of their pattern. Decide together with the children how to arrange the patterns on the display board.

If you have managed to collect some tartan clothes, the children can help to arrange them on the display table and write labels for each article.

Discussion

How many different patterns can you see in the display? Are there any that match? Look at the picture of a person in Scottish national costume and ask the children some simple questions. What is the person wearing? Encourage the children to learn and use the correct words for the things they can see in the picture, such as kilt, sporran, gaiter and buckles. Talk about each family having its own special tartan. Which tartan would the children choose for their own family? Do they know the names of any tartans?

A SUNNY DAY

What you need

A print of *Sunday Afternoon on the Isle of Grand Jatte* by George Pierre Seurat (1859-91), sky blue backing paper, the children's original drawings and enlarged paintings (from the activity on page 20), coloured and shiny paper, lace, ribbons, wool, sequins, doilies, green tissue paper, plate stands, a display board and table, white paper (A3 and A4), dark blue paper, sky blue crêpe paper, a staple gun, scissors, PVA glue, some viewfinders, the 'I Spy' list (from the activity on page 20), a lacy parasol (optional).

Preparation

Cover the display board in sky blue paper. Cut each sheet of white A4 paper into two cloud shapes. Cover the table in scrunched-up green tissue paper. Mount the children's drawings and paintings (see page 20) on dark blue paper. Cut the coloured and shiny paper into A4-sized pieces. Cut out a large cloud shape from white A3 paper and label neatly with the title 'Sunday Afternoon on the Isle of Grand Jatte by George Pierre Seurat'. Hang this on two strips of crêpe paper pinned to the ceiling slightly in front of the display board.

What to do

Make a border with the small cloud shapes. Place the print of the Seurat painting in the bottom left-hand corner and arrange the children's drawings and paintings around it. Add clear name labels written by the children. Look carefully at the print to find the ladies' fans and demonstrate how to make fans, from the coloured and shiny paper sheets. Decorate a sheet either by colouring in or drawing patterns. Fold it into a concertina shape (adult help may be needed) and add further decoration such as lace or doilies and sequins. Tie at the bottom with ribbon, perhaps adding a tassel made from wool.

Display the fans on the green tissue paper using plate stands for support. Prop the parasol (if used) on the right-hand side of the table. Use a loop of ribbon and a staple gun to support it by the handle. Write clear labels about the methods used to make their drawings and paintings and mount these onto the display. Place a small box with viewfinders on the table and display the 'I Spy' list.

Discussion

Invite another group of children or parents to look at your display. What can they see in the Seurat picture? Encourage the children to describe their work and the things they found in the picture.

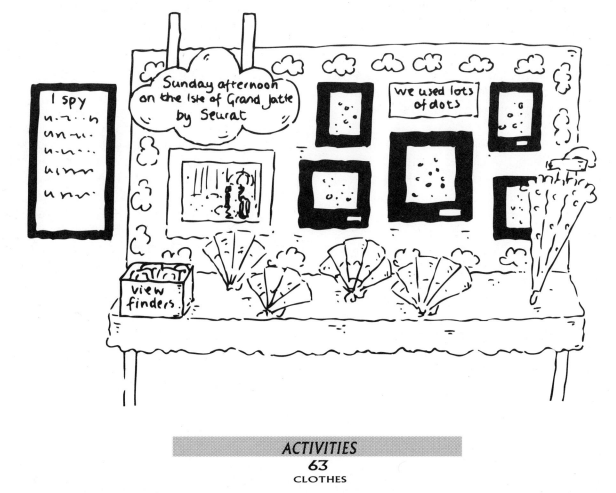

CHAPTER 8
ASSEMBLIES

This chapter suggests ideas for assemblies or group sharing times on the theme of 'Clothes' and includes activities, prayers and songs.

CLOTHES FOR SPECIAL OCCASIONS

In this assembly, children can draw on experiences they may have had during some of the activities related to this topic. They should have begun to appreciate that many people have particular clothes which they wear only on specific occasions. This should help them to develop a future understanding of the place of religious dress within Christianity and the other principal world faiths.

Introduction

Begin by inviting the children to identify some of the key moments in their own lives and those of their families and friends. Perhaps it was their birthday party, or their first day at school. Ask them to recall the clothes worn at these special times. Support their descriptions with pictures, written descriptions or even the garments themselves.

Summarise by reminding the children that the wearing of distinctive clothes is often a way of showing that some occasions have special significance.

What to do

Gather some outfits which, if possible, represent a variety of religious traditions and reflect a range of life events. The selection might include christening or baptismal robes, First Holy Communion dresses, wedding clothes and a prayer shawl and skull cap for a Bar Mitzvah boy. (Contact parents and local religious leaders for help, or alternatively, use posters and slides.)

Explain to the children that people from different faith communities may mark key events in their lives with religious ceremonies which require them to wear distinctive clothes. Invite children to come forward and model the outfits from your collection, accompanied by appropriate music from a range of cultures and faiths. Commentate on the symbolism and importance of these clothes.

Reflection

Invite the clothes 'models' to stand in the centre of the assembly area and focus a spotlight on them. Play a piece of reflective music quietly in the background and encourage the children to think of outfits they may have worn for special occasions. Remind them that these clothes were not significant in themselves, but served as a sign that something important was taking place.

Prayer

Some children may wish to ask God to be with them in all the key moments of their lives, whether happy or sad. Any suitable prayers composed by the children themselves could be read out or displayed on an overhead projector. Formal prayers taken from some of the religious ceremonies described during the 'modelling session' could also be included.

Song

As the children leave, play a recording of 'The Model' by Kraftwerk or invite them to sing a suitable song such as 'Poor Jenny sits a-weeping' on page 84.

JUDGING BY APPEARANCES

This assembly offers children an opportunity to consider whether or not it is appropriate to make judgements about a person on account of the clothes she/he is wearing.

In a world where material success is highly valued and stylish dress is seen to be important, many young children already have a highly developed sense of fashion and demand a wide range of clothing to suit every occasion. In this assembly, children are encouraged to explore the importance of valuing an individual for his/her personal qualities, rather than by appearance.

Introduction

Open the gathering with a selection of songs on the theme of 'Clothes' taken from this book or a range of other sources. Begin by inviting the children to share with one another some examples of the work they have done as part of their 'Clothes' topic. They could show paintings, drawings, graphs of clothes sizes and results of simple experiments with fabric, as well as reciting and performing a selection of appropriate poems and rhymes.

What to do

Ask a group of children to present a short, pre-prepared role play which is loosely based on the parable of 'The Good Samaritan'. Carefully chosen costumes and props will, of course, be necessary! Present the scenario as follows: a man/woman is walking down a street and is attacked by a couple of passers-by. He/she is robbed and left lying at the side of the road. The first person who walks by is a well-dressed businesswoman, but she ignores the injured figure as she is on her way to an important meeting. The second passer-by is a young man in his smart school uniform, but he also walks by as he is on his way to an interview. The third person is less conventionally dressed – perhaps a tramp, a punk or a scruffy child – but this person is the one who helps.

As the story is being told, pause at the relevant points to ask the children what kind of people would wear the clothes in each case. Use this discussion to challenge stereotypes relating to dress.

Reflection

Darken the room and show a series of slides or OHPs which depict people in different styles of dress and invite the children to suggest words to describe their personalities. Remind them that it is how people behave that is really important, not the way they look.

Prayer

Some children may wish to thank God for all the people who have helped them and shown them kindness, particularly those that they disliked at first because of their appearance. It may also be appropriate for some children to offer prayers of their own in gratitude for the clothes they have.

Song

End the gathering with the traditional song 'When I needed a neighbour' which addresses the key themes of the story.

THE PRAYER SHAWL

The focus of this assembly is the book *Always Adam* by Sheldon Oberman and Ted Lewin (Puffin) (see page 96). The story tells of several generations of a Jewish family and the relationships between them. Though simply told, this beautifully illustrated story is rich in meaning and explores the themes of change and continuity through the motif of a Jewish prayer shawl.

The assembly will help children begin to understand the ways in which some things change while others remain the same. It will also introduce them to ritual dress within the Jewish tradition.

Introduction

As the children enter the room, play some appropriate background music which reflects the Jewish theme of this gathering. (See addresses on page 96.) Begin by inviting them to consider all those times when it is necessary to wear special clothes. Let some children model relevant outfits — examples might include a football strip, a Brownie uniform, a swimsuit. Alternatively, show pictures or paintings created by the children.

Remind the children that certain activities require a certain style of dress and that the same is true for religious activities. Show the children a Jewish prayer shawl. If possible, invite a Jewish parent or friend to talk about the shawl's relevance. If this is not an option, the leader of the gathering will have to take on this responsibility! It is important to emphasise that the shawl is worn for prayer by men and boys in the Jewish tradition, and symbolises the way in which they are 'wrapped' in prayer and 'wrapped' in their relationship with God.

What to do

Read the book *Always Adam*. If the group is small, simply use the text itself, making sure that all the children can see the illustrations easily. For a larger group, display the illustrations as OHP transparencies or prepare various children to act out the story with appropriate props and costumes. Emphasise those elements within the story which remain constant and which are passed on from one generation to the other.

Reflection

As the story comes to an end, place the prayer shawl carefully on a table in the centre of the group. Make sure that the table is attractively presented, perhaps covered with a blue cloth and including other Jewish artefacts within the display (see page 96 for details). It may also be appropriate to include one OHP transparency from the book as a backdrop to the table.

Take several candles and place them on the table, lighting them in silence. Invite the children to spend a few quiet moments thinking about the story and to reflect on what changed within it and what remained the same. Encourage them to think about any similarities with their own experiences.

Prayer

Some children may wish to listen to a prayer. A Jewish visitor or colleague might be willing to recite a prayer from Jewish tradition in English or Hebrew, but if this is not possible, a prayer could be offered by the leader or the children themselves. Suitable themes would include change, continuity and the relationships between different generations.

Song

Conclude the gathering with more recorded Jewish music or invite those who wish to join in a traditional Jewish song, such as 'Shalom'.

Collective worship in schools

The assemblies outlined here are suitable for use with children in nurseries and playgroups, but would need to be adapted for use with pupils at registered schools. As a result of legislation enacted in 1944, 1988 and 1993, there are now specific points to be observed when developing a programme of Collective Acts of Worship in a school. Further guidance will be available from your local SACRE — Standing Advisory Council for RE.

POEMS AND RHYMES

GETTING DRESSED

(Sing this to beat. Speed up gradually to catch children out.)

Put your hat on your head
    on your head
    on your head

    Put your shoes on your feet
        on your feet
        on your feet I said

Put your hat on your head
    on your head
    on your head

    Put your shoes on your feet
        on your feet
        on your feet I said

Put your hat on your head
    on your head
    on your head

    Put your jumper on your back
        on your back
        on your back I said

Put your hat on your head
    on your head
    on your head

    Put your scarf on your neck
        on your neck
        on your neck I said

Put your hat on your head
    on your head
    on your head

Repeat using other items of clothes (ie belt on your waist; trousers on your legs; ribbon on your hair).

Brenda Williams

LET'S DO THE FLIP-FLOP FROLIC!

Pop on a flip-flop,
flip on a flop-plip,
flop on a plip-plop,
flick on a flop-flip,

and...

hop-along
pop-along
flounce-along
bounce-along
prance-along
dance-along
into
    the...
        SPLASH!

Judith Nicholls

SECOND BEST

I never get anything new.
With three older brothers,
My clothes come from others.
Does this ever happen to you?

Ian Larmont

GROWN OUT OF

My trousers are tight,
they just won't fit.

And my jumper?
I've grown out of it.

My shirt's too short,
it just won't do.

There are holes in my socks
where my toes push through.

It's lucky I don't
grow out of my skin.
'Cos then there'd be *nothing*
to put me in!

Tony Mitton

PICKING UP THE CLOTHES

Pick your jeans and T-shirt up!
There's a hook behind the door.

Your jumper's getting trodden on!
Please put it in the drawer.

And take those trainers off the bed –
They SHOULD be on the floor!

Sue Cowling

CLUMSY GIANT GETS UP

Clumsy Giant
got out of bed.
He looked for his slippers
and bumped his head.

He went to the bathroom
to wash his face,
spilled soap and water
all over the place.

He looked for his clothes
with a grumbly frown.
Then he put on his T-shirt
upside down.

He scrabbled about
with a grumbly sound
and put on his boots
the wrong way round.

He clomped to the mirror
to brush his hair,
tripped on the carpet
and fell on a chair.

He squeezed his foot
and he rubbed his head.
'I'll try to be careful now,'
he said.

So he got up slowly
and made for the door,
tripped on his bootlace
and fell on the floor.

Tony Mitton

OLD JOHN MUDDLECOMBE

Old John Muddlecombe lost his cap,
(put hands on head)
He couldn't find it anywhere, the poor old chap,
(look for your hat)
He walked down the High Street and everybody said,
(walk slowly round in a circle)
Silly John Muddlecombe you've got it on your head!
(shake your finger and put your hands on your head)

Traditional

SHOES

(Read to a beat, gradually increasing speed. Shout last line.)

Soft shoes, hard shoes
Old shoes too.
Pumps, wellingtons,
a ballet shoe.

Trainers, slippers,
and flip-flop.
Shoes that jump and
shoes that hop.

Lace-ups, Velcro,
buckles galore.
School shoes, sandals,
clogs and more.

Walking boots, football boots
just like mine.
Scruffy shoes, shabby shoes,
shoes that shine.

Red shoes, blue shoes,
shoes that squeak.
Black shoes, brown shoes,
shoes that leak.

Your shoes, my shoes,
quite a few.
But, best of all
MY SHOES ARE NEW!

Brenda Williams

HOW DID YOUR MUM DO THE WASHING, GRAN?

How did your Mum do the washing, Gran,
If she didn't have a washing-machine?
How did your Mum do the washing, Gran?
How did she get the clothes clean?

She boiled all the whites in a copper, Sue.
A copper was a kind of tub.
And all the rest she washed by hand.
She would rub and rub and rub.

Then, she rinsed the clothes in the sink, Sue.
She pushed and pulled them about.
She rinsed the clothes with her hands
To get all the soap suds out.

Then, she put the clothes through a mangle.
Which had two wooden rollers, Sue.
The mangle squeezed the water out
Of the clothes as you wound them through.

Then, she pegged the clothes on the washing-line
With pegs called dolly pegs, Sue.
That's how my Mum washed the clothes, dear,
That's what she used to do.

John Foster

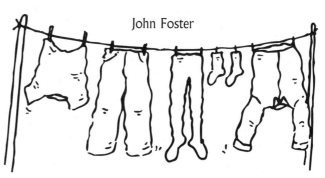

PHOTOCOPIABLE RESOURCES

LOST SOCK

(A counting rhyme)

One shirt a-swishing in the washing machine,
two sweaters swirling in the suds, getting clean,
three slacks a-slapping on the sides of the drum,
four skirts a-spinning with a space-ship hum,
five socks a-sobbing on the line, drip, drip,
for the sixth sock was missing. It had given them the slip.

Gina Douthwaite

SOCKS

Socks have tops
And heels and toes,
Some are plain
And some have bows!
Some have special
Non-slip soles.
They come in pairs
And go in holes!

Sue Cowling

LET'S KEEP OUT THE RAIN

Can I go out in the rain today
Can I go out in the rain?
Put on my wellies like shiny jellies
Splash in the puddles again.

Can I go out in the rain today
Can I go out in the rain?
Put on my mack so shiny and black
Put on my wellies like shiny jellies
Splash in the puddles again.

Can I go out in the rain today
Can I go out in the rain?
Put on my head my hat so red
Put on my mack so shiny and black
Put on my wellies like shiny jellies
Splash in the puddles again.

Can I go out in the rain today
Can I go out in the rain?
Put up my brolly so bright and jolly
Put on my head my hat so red
Put on my mack so shiny and black
Put on my wellies like shiny jellies
Splash in the puddles again.

Maureen Warner

WHO AM I?

My shoes are green,
My socks are red.
A purple hat
sits on my head.

My coat is pink,
my vest is black.
Six silver stars
shine on my back.

My gloves are gold,
my shorts are brown.
So, who am I?

A circus clown!

Wes Magee

SPECIAL CLOTHES FOR SPECIAL PEOPLE

I'm a famous footballer
as everybody knows.
My shirt has stripes across my chest
These are my special clothes.
My shorts have stripes that go down here,
My socks come to my knees.
I wear these boots to help me kick.
My special clothes are these.

I'm a weightless astronaut
As everybody knows.
I pull my shiny spacesuit on,
These are my special clothes.
I put my helmet on my head.
My boots won't let me freeze.
My hands go in my big warm gloves.
My special clothes are these.

I'm a laughing policeman
As everybody knows.
I wear a dark blue uniform,
These are my special clothes.
I have my walkie-talkie here,
'Now move along there, please!'
I always wear my policeman's hat
My special clothes are these.

Stevie Ann Wilde

BURGER BAR GIRL

Girl in a cap
Striped red and white,
Girl in overalls
That dry overnight,
Your clothes are modern
And your smile is bright!

Girl in an apron
Ironed flat,
Girl in a black dress
And little starched hat,
When your Gran was young
She looked like that!

Sue Cowling

OLD CLOTHES

(Can be sung to the tune of 'There was a Princess long ago'; children could walk round, holding hands in a circle.)

Oh, I like wearing old clothes,
  old clothes, old clothes.
Oh, I like wearing old clothes,
  because I feel so free.

I wear them in the garden,
  the garden, the garden.
I wear them in the garden,
  and playing by the sea.

They feel all nice and comfy,
  and comfy, and comfy.
They feel so nice and comfy,
  and still fit me.

You can keep your new clothes,
your new clothes, your new clothes.
You can keep your new clothes,
  they don't suit me.

Jan Pollard

PHOTOCOPIABLE RESOURCES

FIVE ROYAL KNIGHTS

Five royal knights came riding,
in their shining armour,
One fell off his horse, so then there were four.

Four royal knights came riding,
around the big oak tree,
One lost his helmet, so then there were three.

Three royal knights came riding,
in their tunics red and blue,
One broke his sword, so then there were two.

Two royal knights came riding,
to the tournament for some fun,
One dropped his shield, so then there was one.

One royal knight came riding,
and the people shout and cheer (hurrah)
He was the best knight, that was very clear !

Anne Piper

MY JUMPER

My jumper
is all
that a jumper
should be.
It's warm
and it's woolly
and friendly
to me.

It's ragged
and fraying
and falling
to bits.
But I can't
throw it out
for it
perfectly
fits.

My jumper
is all
that a jumper
should be.
It's mine
and it's magic
and special
to me.

Tony Mitton

PSSST!

*Have you seen
Mrs Moggett's knickers
hanging on the line?*

Long, not tiny ones,
pink ones, shiny ones,
baggy ones and dotty ones,
yellow-striped and spotty ones,
giant-sized roomy ones,
blown-up-like-balloon-y ones...
parachute-to-Paris
or take-you-to-the-Moon-y ones...
Have you seen
Mrs Moggett's knickers
swinging on the line?

*(Pssst! Don't all shout,
but Monday's when they're out!)*

Judith Nicholls

STORIES

THE EMPEROR'S NEW CLOTHES

Long ago, there lived an emperor who really *loved* new clothes. He had clothes for the morning and clothes for the afternoon. And he had extra special clothes for the evening. In fact, he had so many clothes that he sometimes didn't know *what* to wear.

One day, two wicked men came to the palace to see the Emperor.

'We are weavers,' they said. 'But we are no ordinary weavers. We can make a special, magic cloth. If a foolish person looks at our cloth, he can't see it at all.'

The Emperor was impressed. This certainly *was* something new.

'I would like you to make me a suit of this magic cloth,' he said eagerly.

The weavers smiled at each other.

'We shall need a very great deal of gold thread,' they said.

'You shall have all the thread you require,' replied the Emperor.

The wicked weavers took all the gold thread and hid it in their bags. Then they sat down and busily pretended to make the magic cloth.

One night, the Emperor wondered how the weavers were getting on.

'Prime Minister, find out if my magic cloth is ready,' he ordered.

Clickety clack, clickety clack, the weavers were hard at work.

'Oh dear,' thought the Prime Minister. 'I can't see a thing, but I know that *I* am not stupid.'

So he hurried off to tell the Emperor that he had never seen such beautiful cloth.

When the Prime Minister had gone, the weavers laughed and laughed. Then they went to the Emperor.

'It is time to sew the cloth into a suit,' they announced. 'We need more gold thread.' When they got the thread, they hid it as before.

The weavers pretended to cut and sew for a whole week. At last they asked the Emperor to try on his new suit.

When he had taken off his clothes, the weavers fussed around the Emperor. 'What a perfect fit!' they both cried.

The Emperor looked in the mirror. He couldn't see any suit at all, but he didn't want to seem foolish.

'It's a beautiful suit,' he said. 'Magnificent!'

The two weavers held their breath until they were sure the Emperor had gone. Then they laughed and laughed and laughed. How was it possible for clever people to be so silly?

By now everyone in the land had heard about the Emperor's new suit. They were all sure that they would be able to see it.

Soon a royal proclamation was sent out. The Emperor was to lead a grand procession, and he would be wearing his new clothes!

When the great day arrived, the Emperor sent for the weavers to help him get dressed.

'Your Highness looks perfect!' they cried when they had finished. But the Emperor still couldn't see the clothes at all.

'I can't be more foolish than the Prime Minister,' he thought, 'and he could see the cloth.' So he paid the weavers handsomely.

The trumpets blew and the great procession started. People had come from far and near to get a good view of the Emperor in his new clothes. But how surprised they were when they saw him!

At last one of the crowd said timidly, 'The Emperor's new clothes are beautiful!'

Then everyone started talking at once. 'So fashionable!' 'Very smart!' 'Divine!' they said, each of them anxious not to seem more foolish than the rest.

But one small boy laughed out loud and shouted, 'Look! The Emperor has no clothes on!'

At once the people around him began to laugh as well.

'Oh no!' gasped the Emperor, turning very red. 'I have been the most foolish person of all!'

As for the weavers, they were nowhere to be seen!

Retold by Audrey Daly. Based on the story by Hans Christian Andersen

SUNDAY BOOTS AND WORKING BOOTS

In a cupboard under the stairs of a little cottage lived two pairs of boots. Their names were Sunday Boots and Working Boots. They belonged to a man called Dad.

'Missus,' he said to his wife on Sunday mornings, 'have you seen my Sunday boots?'

'Yes, Dad,' Mum answered. 'They're under the stairs all cleaned and polished, ready to wear to church.'

On hearing this, Sunday Boots gleamed wickedly in the dim light of the cupboard.

'See, you dirty old working boots,' they said. 'We are off to church. Only the best boots are worn to church. You will never be worn to church. You are much too old and dirty!'

Sunday Boots, although smart and shiny, were not nice at all. In fact, they were very nasty, particularly to Working Boots.

Dad was a farmer, and he wore Working Boots whilst he worked in the fields from Mondays to Saturdays. The fields were muddy, and the mud stuck to Working Boots. This happened so often that Dad said to Missus, 'It's not worth cleaning my old working boots because they will only get covered in mud again tomorrow.'

So Working Boots got dirtier and dirtier, muddier and muddier, and Sunday Boots hissed, 'Get away from us, you filthy boots! We don't want you spoiling our shiny black polish! We can't understand why Dad puts you in the cupboard with us.'

'We're sorry,' said Working Boots sadly, 'but we can't help being muddy.'

Sunday Boots stuck their tongues out at Working Boots and said rudely, 'Be quiet. We are going to sing. We are going to sing one of the beautiful songs we hear when we are in church.'

And they sang *All Things Bright and Beautiful.*

'That was lovely, Sunday Boots,' said Working Boots. 'You do sing well.'

'Of course,' Sunday Boots said grandly. 'But then we are of the very best leather. We doubt if dirty things like you can sing, even if you know any songs.

'Oh, we know one song,' said Working Boots eagerly. 'Dad sings it when we are out in the fields. It goes like this.'

They began to sing sweetly *My Old Man's a Dustman.*

'Stop! Stop!' shrieked Sunday Boots. 'What a dreadfully common song, and what dreadfully common voices!'

They turned on their heels and settled themselves in the corner of the cupboard as far away from Working Boots as they could get.

One day, as Dad was pulling on Working Boots ready for work, Missus said, 'Dad, those old boots of yours are quite worn out. You'll have to buy some more.'

Dad nodded his head. 'Yes, you're right, Missus. There are two great holes in them that are quite past mending.'

Working Boots were horrified.

'Whatever is going to happen to us?' they whispered fearfully to Sunday Boots when they were put away for the night.

'Why, don't you know?' sneered Sunday Boots. 'You won't be needed any more. You'll be thrown away and you'll be able to sing *My Old Man's a Dustman* all the way to the dump where they put all the rest of the rubbish.'

Working Boots felt sad and frightened. They did not feel much happier when, next day, Dad took Sunday Boots out of the cupboard and, although it was not yet Sunday, put them on to wear to the shops. All day long Working Boots stood by themselves in the cupboard.

'Oh dear,' they sighed, 'we really don't want to be thrown onto the rubbish dump. We like it here, even if Sunday Boots are so horrible to us.'

Great tears fell from their lace holes.

When Dad and Missus came home, Dad placed a brand new pair of boots in the cupboard. He picked up Working Boots and took them into the backyard. He was just about to throw them into the dustbin when he said, 'You know, Missus, these old boots have been very good to me all these years. It seems a shame to throw them away.' Suddenly, he smiled and said, 'I don't think I will throw them away. I've an idea.'

Dad carried Working Boots to his workshed and closed the door behind him.

Some time later, Dad came into the kitchen and beamed at Missus. He held out Working Boots. They were no longer dirty, but sparkling clean. Dad has brushed them thoroughly and given them a good coating of varnish. And in them he had planted two beautiful geraniums.

'My, my,' Missus said in delight, 'those boots make lovely plant pots. They will look just right on my kitchen window-sill.'

Working Boots were overjoyed. From that day onwards they sat on the sill proudly holding their geraniums.

And what did Dad wear now when he went out to work in the fields?

Well, of course he did not want to spoil his smart new boots. So he wore Sunday Boots for work from Monday to Saturday. And soon they became muddy. Very muddy indeed.

Annette Penny

THE RED SOCK

Holly had socks of all different colours, but her favourite were a red pair with white bows at the top. Every time she had to go somewhere special, or needed cheering up, she wore her red socks.

Then, one day, something terrible happened.

While Holly's mum was hanging out the washing, their young puppy, Coco, grabbed a red sock out of the basket and ran off with it. By the time Holly had found him, the sock was chewed to pieces.

Holly was very upset.

'Oh dear,' said Holly's mum. 'We'll have to throw those socks away now and get you a new pair.' She went to put them both in the bin, but Holly stopped her.

'Please let me keep the good one, Mum,' she said.

'One sock's not much use, Holly,' her mum replied, but handed her the single red sock. Holly took it up to her room and put it safely in the drawer.

At first Holly took the red sock out every day and looked at it, wishing she still had the other one so she could wear them again. After a while, though, Mum bought her a new pair – bright pink with lacy tops – and the red sock was gradually pushed to the back of the drawer, unworn and forgotten.

Then, one day, Holly woke up with a really sore throat. She was very hot. The doctor said she must stay in bed for a couple of days and rest. Her mum tried to make her feel better, with a new comic and her favourite fruit juice, but Holly was very fed up and miserable.

As her mum put away Holly's clothes for her that morning, she saw the red sock in Holly's drawer. It gave her an idea. While Holly slept, her mum took out her sewing box, picked up the red sock, and began to sew...

'Hello, Holly!' said a strange, squeaky voice.

Holly sleepily opened her eyes and stared in surprise. A cheery little red face looked straight at her from the side of the bed and tossed its woolly hair about.

'Do you feel like coming to play?' it squeaked.

'Sock!' cried Holly. 'It's you!' And she laughed as the sock ran backwards and forwards beside the bed, pretending to sneeze like Holly.

'*Achoo!*' sneezed the sock. 'Dow you've given be your cold!'

Then she heard her Mum laughing, so Holly leant over the side of the bed and saw her Mum sitting on the floor, with the red sock over her hand.

'Here,' she said to Holly, 'you have it. I'm too old for this kind of game!'

Laughing still, she peeled off the sock puppet she had made and gave it to Holly, who was delighted. 'Oh, Mum, it's great! Thank you ever so much,' said Holly, putting the puppet over her hand.

As Holly's mum left the bedroom, she turned and watched Holly playing with the sock puppet and talking to it. Suddenly, being stuck in bed and poorly wasn't half so bad.

The red sock never went back into the drawer again. It stayed next to Holly's bed and was her best toy ever.

Karen King

PHOTOCOPIABLE RESOURCES

THE ELVES AND
THE SHOEMAKER

A long time ago, there once was a poor shoemaker. He was very good at making shoes, but the town where he lived had so many other shoemakers, that he never managed to sell enough shoes to feed his family.

Soon, he had only one small piece of leather left, and no money to buy any more.

'I can't make shoes without leather,' she said to his wife. 'And if I have no shoes to sell, we won't have any money to buy food. I just don't know what to do!'

'Well,' said his wife, 'you must make one last pair of shoes, then.'

The shoemaker did as his wife said. He carefully cut a pair of shoes from the leather, but it took him so long he did not have time to sew the pieces together that night. So he left everything tidily on his work bench ready for the morning.

The next day, when he came back to his workroom, he saw an amazing sight. Sitting on his workbench was the most beautiful pair of shoes he had ever seen! The stitches were so small, he could hardly see them, and the seams were so smooth they would never rub. The shoemaker held them in his trembling hands.

'Who could have made these?' he asked himself.

He put the shoes in his shop window. Straight away, a rich gentleman came in and bought them. Now the shoemaker had some money for food and more leather.

All day long he worked, cutting out shoes of different shapes, styles and sizes, until he was too tired to work any more. He left everything on his bench tidy for the morning, and went home.

When he returned the next morning, the shoemaker found that once again all his work had been done for him. All the pieces he'd left the night before had been sewn together perfectly, into the most wonderful shoes he'd ever seen.

Once again, he put the shoes in his shop window.

By the time he shut the shop that evening, all the shoes had been sold.

Day after day, the shoemaker cut out shoes and during the night someone came and finished them for him. He didn't know who it was, but they were surely the best shoemakers in the world.

The shoemaker's shop became famous and the shoemaker became very rich.

Just before Christmas, the shoemaker had an idea.

PHOTOCOPIABLE RESOURCES

He said to his wife, 'I think we should stay up tonight and find out just who is helping us!'

So that's what they did. They hid in the workroom and waited, trying hard not to sneeze, or cough, or make a sound.

At midnight they heard the sound of tiny feet, like mice, running across the floor. But it wasn't mice they saw: it was two tiny men! The shoemaker and his wife watched, amazed, as the little men climbed up onto the workbench and set to work with needles as big as themselves and reels of thread that were even bigger.

'Elves!' whispered the shoemaker to his wife. '*Elves* have been helping us!'

'Just look at the poor things,' said his wife. 'Their clothes are rags! They must be cold. Husband, we must make them some clothes!'

The elves had given them so much help, it seemed the right thing to do.

The next day the shoemaker and his wife bought some small pieces of fabric and some soft leather. All week the wife cut and sewed, making the most perfect little suits she could, with her neatest stitches. Her husband made two pairs of tiny shoes.

On Christmas Eve they finished the gifts, wrapped them up and left them on the workbench. Then they hid themselves once more, to watch the elves open their presents.

At midnight, just as before, the elves ran across the floor and on to the workbench. When they saw the parcels, they fell on them with great excitement and unwrapped them as fast as they could. Coloured paper and string flew about the workroom.

They held up the little suits and squealed with delight. Then they put on the clothes and shoes and danced about in them joyfully, admiring each other.

'Brother,' said one of the little men,' we can't work in these beautiful clothes – we'll spoil them!'

'I shall never work again,' said the other, 'not now I'm so well dressed!'

The two elves hugged each other with glee, jumped down from the bench and ran away into the night, never to be seen again.

But the shoemaker was now so famous for his wonderful shoes, that many people continued to come to his shop. His stitches may not have been quite so small, nor his seams quite so smooth, but no-one noticed. He and his family were never poor again.

Retold from the Brothers Grimm by Jackie Andrews in the Favourite Tales series (Ladybird).

PHOTOCOPIABLE RESOURCES

SONGS

HOORAY FOR CLOTHES

1. Stand up if you're wear-ing socks to-day, stand up if you're wear-ing socks. Stand up and wave your arms a-bout, but on-ly if you're wear-ing socks.

Chorus
Ya Hoo! Touch your toes turn a-round and a-round, Jump up and down and touch your toes and shout HOO-RAY! for clothes.

Subsequent verse suggestions:

shirt, skirt or dress, trousers, jumper,
hat, watch, earrings, shoes.

Belinda Morley

SPARKLING JEWELS FOR SALE

Chorus

| E♭ | B♭7 | E♭ | A♭ | B♭7 | E♭ |

Shin - y sil - ver, glit - ter - ing gold, Spark - ling jewels, new and old.

| E♭ | B♭7 | F | F7 | B♭ | B♭7 |

Play 4 times

1. Bang - les and brace - lets, my, oh, my! Bang - les and brace - lets, come and buy.____

Last Chorus

| E♭ | B♭7 | E♭ | A♭ | B♭7 | E♭ |

Shin - y sil - ver, glit - ter - ing gold, Spark - ling jewels, new and old.

Verse 2. Brooches and pins oh, my, oh, my.
Brooches and pins do come and buy.
Chorus
Verse 3. Pendants and chokers oh, my, oh, my.
Pendants and chokers do come and buy.
Chorus
Verse 4. Earrings and anklets oh, my, oh, my.
Earrings and anklets do come and buy.
Chorus

Ann Bryant

RUB-A-DUB-A-DUB

How did they wash a long, long time a-go? How did they wash a long, long time a-go?

How did they wash a long, long time a-go? 1. They did wash-ing in an old grey tub.
2. Used a dol-ly in the old grey tub.

Scrub, scrub, rub-a-dub-a-dub. 1. Did their wash-ing in an old grey tub. Scrub, scrub,
2. Used a dol-ly in the old grey tub.

1,3. rub-a-dub-a-dub. Got their wash-ing clean. **2,4.** Got their wash-ing clean. *D.C.*

Clive Barnwell

ME AND MY CLOTHES

Me and my clothes, Me and my clothes, We go ev-'ry-where to-ge-ther.

Me and my clothes, Me and my clothes, To-ge-ther what-e-ver the wea-ther.

Johanne Levy

PHOTOCOPIABLE RESOURCES

CLOTHES FOR A COLD DAY

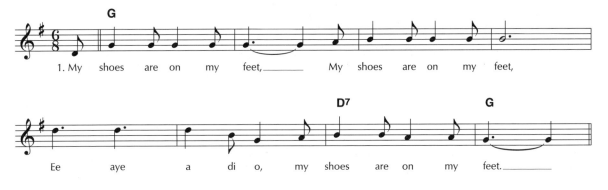

1. My shoes are on my feet,___ My shoes are on my feet,

Ee aye a di o, my shoes are on my feet.___

Verse 2. My coat is on my back, My coat is on my back,
Ee aye a di o, My coat is on my back.
Verse 3. My hat is on my head, My hat is on my head,
Ee aye a di o, My hat is on my head.
Verse 4. My scarf is round my neck, My scarf is round my neck,
Ee aye a di o, My scarf is round my neck.
Verse 5. My gloves are on my hands, My gloves are on my
hands,
Ee aye a di o, My gloves are on my hands.
Verse 6. I'm ready to go out, I'm ready to go out,
Ee aye a di o, I'm ready to go out.

Encourage the children to mime the various actions.

Barbara Moore

PHOTOCOPIABLE RESOURCES

POOR JENNY SITS A-WEEPING

1. Poor Jen - ny sits a - weep - ing, a - weep - ing, a - weep - ing. Poor Jen - ny sits a - weep - ing. On a bright swum - mers day.

Verse 2. Oh why is she a-weeping, a-weeping, a-weeping
She's weeping for a sweetheart, a sweetheart, a sweetheart
Verse 4. Now Jenny choose a sweetheart, a sweetheart, a sweetheart
Verse 5. Now Jenny choose your bridesmaids, your
bridesmaids, your bridesmaids
Verse 6. Now Jenny choose your page boys, your page boys,
your page boys
Verse 7. Now Jenny choose the parson, the parson, the parson
Verse 8. Now Jenny shall be married, be married, be married.

Traditional. Arranged by Peter Morrell

PHOTOCOPIABLE RESOURCES

UNIFORMS

1. Some-one's wear-ing a big white ap-ron, some-one's wear-ing a big white ap-ron,
2. Some-one's wear-ing a big tall hel-met, some-one's wear-ing a big tall hel-met,
3. Some-one's wear-ing a yel-low rain-coat, some-one's wear-ing a yel-low rain-coat,
4. Some-one's wear-ing a bright red sweat-shirt, some-one's wear-ing a bright red sweat shirt,

Some-one's wear-ing a big white ap-ron. Hel-lo, din-ner la-dy.
some-one's wear-ing a big tall hel-met. Hel-lo Mis-ter Police-man.
some-one's wear-ing a yel-low rain-coat. Hel-lo cross-ing la-dy.
some-one's wear-ing a bright red sweat-shirt. Hel-lo * school boy.

Insert the name of your school

Chorus

Un-i-forms say where we come from. Un-i-forms say what we're do-ing.

Un-i-forms tell ev-'ry-bo-dy we be-long to-geth-er.

tune: *The Drunken Sailor*

At * insert the name of your school.

Support the song with pictures of people in uniform, or dress the children up.

Make up more verses using other uniforms the children know about.

Jan Holdstock

MASK MAGIC

Masks are fun, you can be an-y-one, a red-nosed clown or a foot-ball star! Masks are great, you can

make them all wait, un-til you re-veal *(who's un-der that mask)* who you real-ly are!

Spoken:

Sue Nicholls

AIKEN DRUM

1. Oh there was a man lived in the moon, lived in the moon, lived in the moon. There was a man lived in the moon and his name was Ai-ken Drum. And he played up-on a la-dle, a

Chorus

la-dle, a la-dle, He played up-on a la-dle and his name was Ai-ken Drum.

And his hat was made of good cream cheese, good cream cheese, good cream cheese,
And his hat was made of good cream cheese,
And his name was Aiken Drum.

And his coat was made of good roast beef, good roast beef, good roast beef,
And his coat was made of good roast beef,
And his name was Aiken Drum.

And his buttons were made of penny loaves, penny loaves, penny loaves.
And his buttons were made of penny loaves,
And his name was Aiken Drum.

Traditional. Arranged by Peter Morrell

PHOTOCOPIABLE RESOURCES

THE SHOE SHOP

What kind of shoe are you selling at the shoe shop? What kind of shoe have you
trainer, a trainer, I want to buy a trainer. Is there a trainer you've

got for me to wear? What kind of shoe are you selling at the shoe shop?
got for me to wear? A trainer, a trainer, I want to buy a trainer.

1, 2, etc.

Last time

If you've the right ones I will buy a pair. 2. A buy a pair.
If you've a trainer I will buy a pair.

*This can be repeated over and over again using a different
shoe for each verse. For example, sandal, slipper, wellie.*

Clive Barnwell

A BIG BALL OF WOOL

Chorus

We've got a big clap ball clap of wool. clap clap We've got a big clap ball clap of

wool. clap clap So get out the needles, quick quick quick. Let's get knitting, click click click.

1. Now we've got a woolly hat clap clap and a big clap ball clap of wool clap clap

Verse 2. Now we've got a pair of socks.
Verse 3. Now we've got a pair of gloves.
Verse 4. Now we've got a woolly scarf.

Support the song with pictures or real clothes.

Jan Holdstock

PHOTOCOPIABLE RESOURCES

Let's get dressed! (1)

Name _____

Cut out the clothes.
Make sure you stick them on the doll in the right order.

THEMES
for early years

Name _____

Let's get dressed! (2)

Cut out the doll.
Stick on the clothes in the right order.

THEMES
for early years

Name _____

Looking at boots

Match the boots and colour them in.

Name _____

Dress the weather teddy (1)

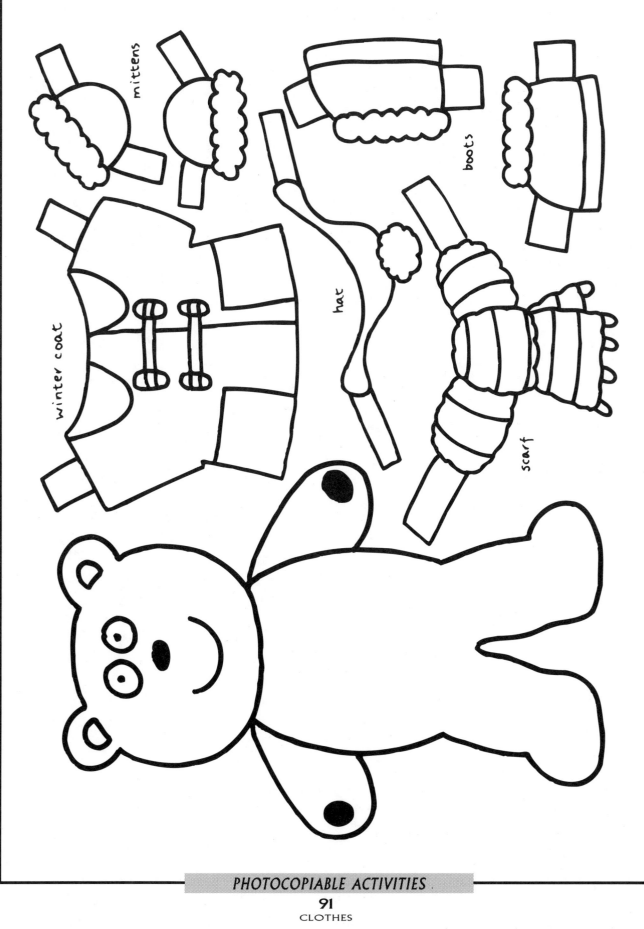

THEMES
for early years

Name _____

Dress the weather teddy (2)

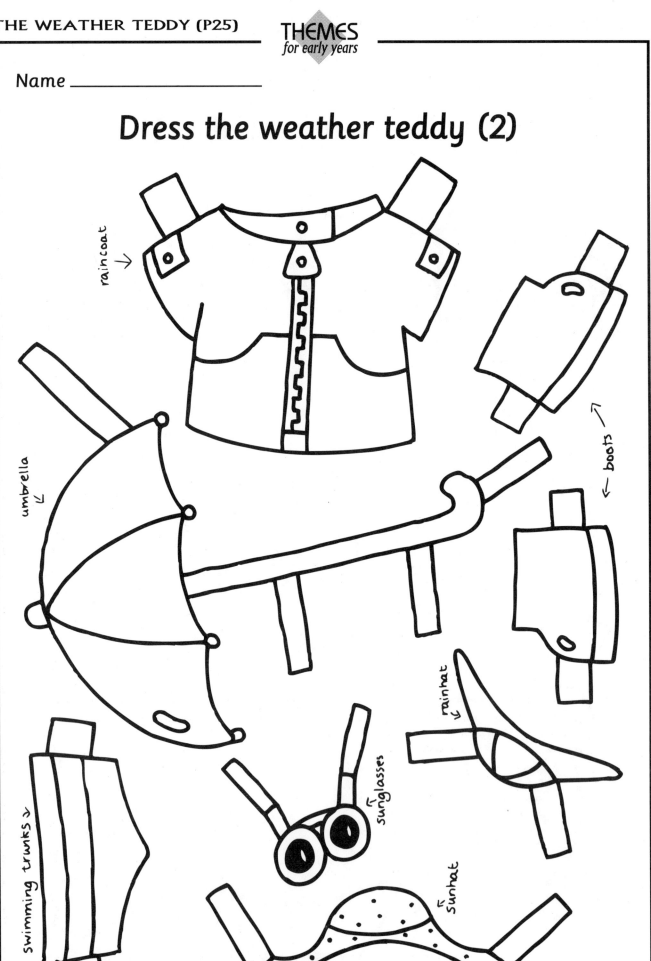

raincoat

boots

umbrella

rainhat

sunglasses

swimming trunks

sunhat

Name _____

The Welsh hat game (1)

You will need 4 scorecards and 40 Welsh hats to play this game.

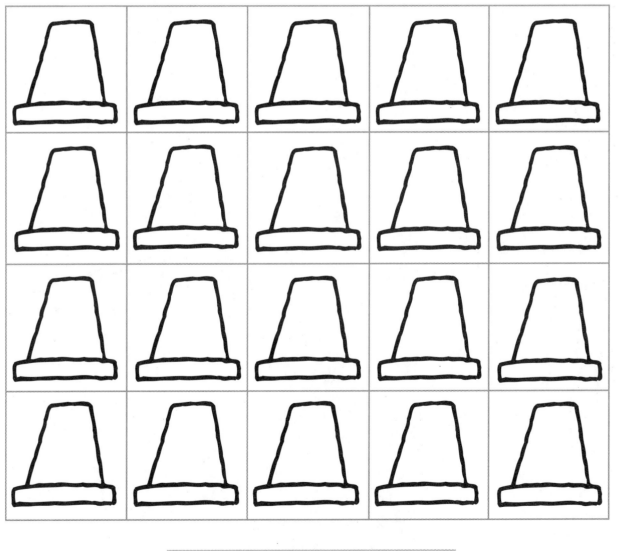

The Welsh hat game (2)

Name _____

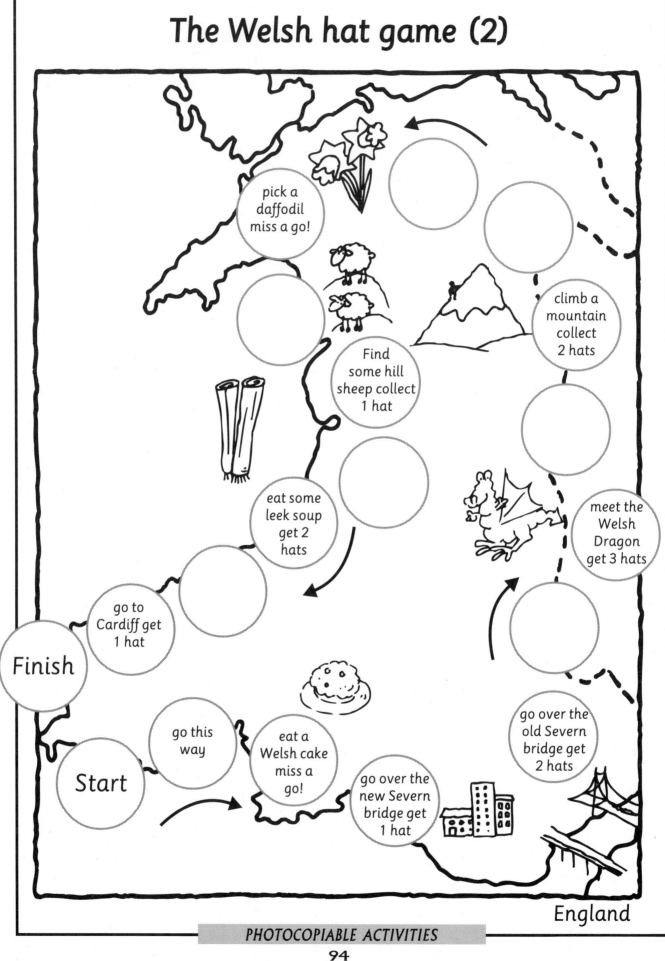

pick a daffodil miss a go!

climb a mountain collect 2 hats

Find some hill sheep collect 1 hat

eat some leek soup get 2 hats

meet the Welsh Dragon get 3 hats

go to Cardiff get 1 hat

Finish

go this way

Start

eat a Welsh cake miss a go!

go over the new Severn bridge get 1 hat

go over the old Severn bridge get 2 hats

England

THEMES
for early years

Match the socks!

THEMES
for early years

RECOMMENDED MATERIALS

SONGS

'I went to the top of the hill' from *Growing with Music* (Longman)

'There was a princess long ago' from *This Little Puffin* (Puffin)

'Johnny get your hair combed' from *BBC Music Box Songbook* (BBC)

'When the Circus comes to town' from *Apusskidu Songs for Children* (A & C Black)

POEMS AND RHYMES

'Happiness' A A Milne from *When We Were Very Young* (Mammoth)

'The King's breakfast' A A Milne from *When We Were Very Young* (Mammoth)

'Miss Polly had a dolly' from *This Little Puffin* (Puffin)

'Sometimes I'm very, very small' from *This Little Puffin* (Puffin)

'Who has seen the wind?' Christina Rosseti (Everyman Poetry)

'Windy day' Linda Hammond from *Five Furry Teddy Bears* (Puffin)

PICTURE AND STORY BOOKS

Always Adam Sheldon Oberman and Ted Lewin (Puffin)

Aldo John Burningham (Red Fox)

Bye Bye Baby Janet and Allan Ahlberg (Little Mammoth)

Cinderella (Traditional)

Doing the Washing Sarah Garland (Puffin)

Emma's Lamb Kim Lewis (Walker Books)

'Foggy Day' from the *Oxford Reading Tree Stage 2* (Oxford University Press)

The Good Samaritan (Bible story)

How do I put it on? Shigeo Watanabe (Red Fox)

The King with Dirty Feet Pomme Clayton (Kingfisher)

The Little Princess Books Tony Ross (Anderson Press)

Making Faces Norman Messenger (Dorling Kindersley)

The Tale of Mrs Tiggy Winkle Beatrix Potter (World International)

Mrs Lather's Laundry by Allan Ahlberg (Penguin)

Mrs Mopple's Washing Line Anita Hewett and and Robert Broomfield (Red Fox)

Mrs Wobble the Waitress Allan Ahlberg (Penguin)

New Boots for Alfie Shirley Hughes (Walker Books)

New Clothes for Alex Mary Dickinson and Charlotte Firmin (Hippo Books)

Noah's Ark (Bible story)

Peepo! Janet and Allan Ahlberg (Penguin)

Penguin Small Mick Inkpen (Hodder Children's Books)

Pinnochio (Traditional)

Postman Pat's Foggy Day John Cunliffe (Hippo Books)

Sleeping Beauty (Traditional)

Smarty Pants Joy Cowley and June Melser *Story Chest* series (Nelson)

So Much T Cooke and H Oxenbury (Walker Books)

Solo: The Little Penguin Paul Geraghty (Hutchinson)

'The King asked the Queen' A A Milne from *When We Were Very Young* (Meuthen)

The Wind Blew Pat Hutchins (Red Fox)

There's No Such Thing as a Dragon Jack Kent (Happy Cat Books)

The Three Billy Goats Gruff (Traditional)

The Very Hungry Caterpillar Eric Carle (Penguin)

USEFUL ADDRESSES

The Jewish Education Bureau, 8 Westcombe Avenue, Leeds, LS 2BS produces a catalogue which includes books, artefacts, videos and cassettes, available to schools/teachers who write enclosing an SAE.

A catalogue of books, Jewish music on tape and CD, Prayer shawls and other Jewish artefacts are available from Manor House Books, 80 East End Road, Finchley, London N3 2SY

Robert Opie Museum of the Label, Old Gloucester Dock, Gloucester

The Shoe Museum, Clarks Village, Street, Somerset

The Snowman video, Raymond Briggs (Palace)

Letter templates available from Galt-Educational, Culvert Street, Oldham, Lancashire

Multicultural and uniforms role-play clothes from Step by Step Ltd, Lavenham Road, Beeches Trading Estate, Yate, Bristol BS37 5QX

PHOTOCOPIABLE RESOURCES